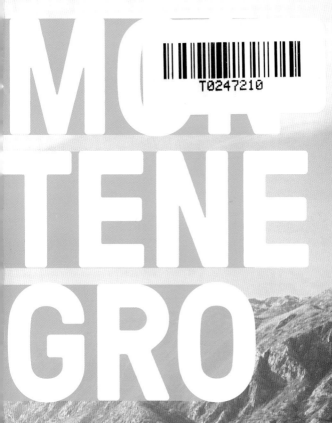

MON
TENE
GRO

Travel with Marco Polo Insider Tips

T0247210

MARCO POLO TOP HIGHLIGHTS

HERCEG NOVI ⭐ **1**
No other place on the Adriatic has more hours of sunshine than Montenegro's "Flower Town".

➤ p. 44, Bay of Kotor

BUDVA OLD TOWN ⭐ **4**
Hundreds of years of history emanate from the thick stone walls and romantic alleyways right on the waterfront.

➤ p. 66, The Adriatic

KOTOR OLD TOWN ⭐ **2**
Time travel to the Middle Ages while strolling past magnificent buildings and making the challenging ascent to the citadel.
📷 *Tip: The rocky trails up to the citadel are illuminated at night, which makes for a great shot from the harbour.*

➤ p. 51, Bay of Kotor

SV. STEFAN ⭐ **5**
Once the island of fishermen, now a luxury hotel – and still an enchanting sight.
📷 *Tip: Leave the car in the car park just before the steep descent and photograph the island from above.*

➤ p. 70, The Adriatic

GOSPA OD ŠKRPJELA ⭐ **3**
This island church in the Bay of Kotor stands on sunken shipwrecks and piled-up boulders.
📷 *Tip: Hire a kayak and photograph the church and its neighbouring island from the water.*

➤ p. 54, Bay of Kotor

VELIKA PLAŽA ⭐ **6**
"Grand Beach" in Ulcinj, the country's longest stretch of sand, is so much more than a paradise for windsurfers.

➤ p. 79, The Adriatic

LAKE SKADAR ⭐ 7
Surrounded by high mountains, the Balkans' biggest lake, *Skadarsko Jezero*, is one of nature's great spectacles.

➤ p. 88, Cetinje, Lake Skadar & Podgorica

DURMITOR NATIONAL PARK ⭐
At more than 2,000m above sea level, glacial lakes, ski slopes and remote forest trails await in this wild and fascinating national park (photo).

➤ p. 104, The Northwest

MANASTIR OSTROG ⭐ 8
The monastery, which is hewn into the rock at great altitude, is a magnet not just for the faithful.
📷 *Stop at the lower monastery, where the switchback road begins and take a photograph of the "eagle's nest" from below.*

➤ p. 101, The Northwest

TARA RIVER CANYON ⭐ 10
For an adrenaline-fuelled adventure, take a trip to Montenegro's longest river and the world's second-deepest canyon.
📷 *Tip: Get a spectacular view of the gigantic bridge from Kljajevića Luka Camp.*

➤ p. 105, The Northwest

CONTENTS

THE NORTHWEST

THE NORTHEAST

BAY OF KOTOR

CETINJE, LAKE SKADAR & PODGORICA

THE ADRIATIC

CONTENTS

⏱	Plan your visit	🍴	Eating/drinking
€-€€€	Price categories	🛍	Shopping
(*)	Premium-rate phone number	🍸	Nightlife
			Top beaches

(*A2*) Refers to the removable pull-out map
(0) Located off the map

Piva River canyon

BEST OF
MONTE-
NEGRO

Fishing island turned celebrity destination: Sv. Stefan

BEST ☂ WHEN IT RAINS

ACTIVITIES TO BRIGHTEN YOUR DAY

SPORT IS KING!

In *Bijela* you can exercise in the gym, and practise tennis, judo or boxing – all nicely under cover if the weather is bad. And if you go scuba diving, it doesn't matter whether it is raining or sunny.

➤ p. 49, Bay of Kotor

PAY HOMAGE TO SEAFARERS

The area around the Bay of Kotor is the birthplace of many famous sea captains who braved the wind and weather on the high seas. You can be inspired by their feats in Kotor's *Maritime Museum*.

➤ p. 51 Bay of Kotor

BRAVE RAINDROPS ON THE SAND

The mild climate of the Adriatic means you can walk barefoot along the beach and have your feet massaged by the wet sand; try it on the *Grand Beach* in Ulcinj.

➤ p. 79, The Adriatic

CENTRE OF MODERN ART

Most Montenegrin artists have a style that is in character with their country. The *Galerija Centar* in Podgorica displays contemporary art that is so full of power, energy and colour that it is impossible to think of the rain outside!

➤ p. 93, Cetinje, Lake Skadar & Podgorica

IN AN ORTHODOX SANCTUARY

The Metropolitan Bishop of Herzegovina had the *Ostrog Monastery* built into the cliff as a place of refuge from the Turks. If you seek shelter from the rain here, you will find peace in the tranquil rooms and fascinating frescoes on the stone walls (photo).

➤ p. 101, The Northwest

BEST

ON A BUDGET

FOR SMALLER WALLETS

UP-&-COMING ARTISTS
This is the place to discover new talent! The *Gallery Josip Bepo Benković* in Herceg Novi exhibits work by young Montenegrin artists, and it costs nothing to look.
➤ p. 45, Bay of Kotor

TAKE THE SCENIC ROAD
The journey will be shorter but you will have to pay 2.50 euros if you drive through the Sozina Tunnel from Lake Skadar to the Montenegrin coast. The alternative route follows the winding *road from Virpazar* to the Adriatic near Petrovac; it is toll free and the panoramic views are spectacular.
➤ p. 63, The Adriatic

OPEN-AIR & LIVE IN BUDVA
There is a small charge to enter the *citadel* of this Adriatic town, but in summer you can enjoy regular free, open-air concerts in an impressive, historic setting.
➤ p. 67, The Adriatic

FREE BENCH AT THE BEACH
A sun lounger on the beach in *Petrovac na Moru* costs 10 euros; but to sit on one of the lovely old benches on the promenade is gratis. You will still have the sand and sea right in front of you and trees to provide shade.
➤ p. 71, The Adriatic

WALK ACROSS THE BRIDGE
You should visit the Tara Canyon even if you aren't keen on adrenaline-pumping activities such as zip-lining or rafting. A walk across the long *Đurđevića Tara Bridge* with its stunning views is absolutely free (photo).
➤ p. 106, The Northwest

BEST WITH CHILDREN

FUN FOR YOUNG & OLD

POWER TO THE CHILDREN

The *International Children's Carnival* is held in June in Herceg Novi, and the colourful costumes will really delight the little ones.

➤ p. 48, Bay of Kotor

DISCOVER YOUR WILD SIDE

A visit to the *Avanturistički Park Lovćen* is a thrilling outdoor experience for kids and their parents. You can climb, slide, crawl and jump over obstacles surrounded by unspoiled nature in the Lovćen Mountains.

➤ p. 86, Cetinje, Lake Skadar & Podgorica

LIFE ON THE PONY FARM

On the outskirts of Podgorica is the *Konjički klub Poni*, a pony-riding club (also offering sessions for beginners) with a petting zoo that includes deer, rabbits and goats.

➤ p. 94, Cetinje, Lake Skadar & Podgorica

CROSS THE ABYSS

At *Durmitor Adventure*, a zip-line stretches for 350m across Europe's deepest canyon, the Tara Gorge, providing an adrenaline rush for people of all ages.

➤ p. 106, The Northwest

HERB HEAVEN

The botanical garden of *Botanička Bašta* in Dulovina near the town of Kolašin has a collection of the region's rare plants. The life's work of Daniel Vincek, the so-called "herb king" of Montenegro, is a small paradise that is fascinating for children and adults alike.

➤ p. 115, The Northeast

DISCOVER MONTENEGRO

Top sights in the Bay of Kotor: the church islands of Gospa od Škrpjela and Sv. Đorđe

Only a few hours' flying time from the UK lies a little holiday paradise: Montenegro, the land of the Black Mountain, with 300km of Adriatic coastline and incredible beaches. The rest of the country is dominated by mountains, which are spectacular, although not particularly high. Raging rivers wind their way through deep canyons and snow-covered peaks are reflected in tiny alpine lakes.

A SMALL COUNTRY PACKED WITH HIGHLIGHTS

It is rare to have so much to see and experience in such a small area: from the most westerly to easterly points in Montenegro is a mere 176km, and the country measures only 200km from north to south. After the Grand Canyon, the Tara River Canyon in the northwest of the country is the second deepest in the world,

Around 1200 BCE
Illyrians settle at Lake Skadar

15th–18th century
Venetian rule of the coastal towns

1815–1918
The Habsburgs control a part of the coast

1878
Montenegro is recognised as a sovereign state for the first time

1918
The country becomes part of the Kingdom of Serbs, Croats and Slovenes

1941
Italian occupation of Montenegro, with partisans fighting the occupiers

and one of the last primeval forests in Europe lies hidden in the highlands of the Biogradska gora National Park. More birds nest on Lake Skadar than on any other lake in Europe, and the only fjord in the Mediterranean lies beneath almost perpendicular rock face between the towns of Herceg Novi and Kotor. From the legendary Lovćen mountain range there are panoramic views all the way to Bosnia, Croatia, Albania and – on a clear day – to Italy.

THE MAGICAL ADRIATIC

Nowhere on the eastern Adriatic has more beautiful sandy beaches than those between Bar and Ulcinj. The idyllic bays hidden behind rocks and backed with pines, cypresses and olive trees are typical of Montenegro's coastline. A stroll through the "flower town" of Herceg Novi, the seafaring hamlet of Perast or across the picturesque hotel island of Sv. Stefan will take you back to the heyday of European architecture. The pedestrian area of Kotor's old town reveals an architectural melange of Venetian Baroque buildings and Austro-Hungarian townhouses. Centuries-old Orthodox monasteries are tucked away further inland.

ALWAYS 100 PER CENT EUROPEAN

The Montenegrins defend their country's multicultural spirit, which continued to flourish here after the collapse of Josip Broz Tito's Socialist Yugoslavia. Croats, Serbs, Albanians, Roma and Muslims have lived alongside each other for centuries – and both the government and opposition of the small republic stress the

1945
Montenegro becomes a part of Yugoslavia

1990s
In 1992, a vast majority votes to remain in Yugoslavia, siding with Serbia in the Yugoslav Wars

2003
Yugoslavia is dissolved and the State Union of Serbia & Montenegro remains

2006
Referendum on independence from Serbia

2017
The country becomes a member of NATO

2021
Montenegro promises reforms in order to apply for EU membership

virtue of this tolerance in their efforts to accede to the European Union. The Montenegrins have no doubt that their country's roots can be found deep in Europe. In Cetinje, the old embassy buildings recall the time when the nine daughters of Tsar Nicholas I married into the major courts of Europe and the wily diplomat became known as the "father-in-law of Europe". Well before that, noble families from Venice to Petersburg had invited Montenegrin artists and captains into their employ. And the European roots sink even deeper: Greeks, Illyrians and Romans settled in the area south of Dubrovnik before the Roman Empire divided its territory at the end of the fourth century.

RISE AND FALL

It was not until the 1960s that the small country was discovered as a holiday destination. And then things really took off for Montenegro, and anybody who had a spare bed rented it to a tourist. Hotels with "beguiling socialist charm" sprang up everywhere. Sv. Stefan, the fishing island carved out of stone, became an exclusive holiday location for celebrities such as Sophia Loren and Michael Douglas. However, the Yugoslav War in the 1990s crippled the economy. Although there was no fighting action in the country itself, Montenegro suffered from the uncertain political situation in the Balkans. Hotels and guesthouses fell into disrepair, poverty once again hit the country that had come to rely so heavily on tourism, and many young university graduates went abroad to find work.

SERBIA AND MONTENEGRO – DOESN'T THAT RING A BELL?

Twenty years ago, many politicians felt that the confederation with Serbia was an obstacle on Montenegro's path into the European Union. Milo Đukanovič, who was president from 1998 to 2002 and Prime Minister several times after that, did everything he could to promote secession. He introduced the euro as the country's currency in 2002 and established borders within the state of Serbia-Montenegro. A narrow majority (55 per cent) voted for independence from Serbia in a referendum. More than a decade after independence, things have still not calmed down. Today, almost 30 per cent of the population continues to identify as Serbian. The feeling of being a Serb is rooted in history. Many Montenegrins regarded Serbia and the former Yugoslavia as their second home. The pro-Serbian opposition in parliament does little to help this. Nevertheless, today Montenegro is and remains an independent state.

For a long time Montenegro struggled with the economic challenges that came with the transition from socialism (as part of the former Yugolslavia) to capitalism, but for several years there has been a gradual upswing. The introduction of the euro attracted many foreign investors to the country, mainly investors in the hotel industry. Many luxury resorts, marinas and golf courses are being built. Then came the pandemic: Montenegro experienced a high number of infections – comparable to other countries in the region.

AT A GLANCE

622,000 inhabitants

Edinburgh: 554,000

260km
of coastline

Isle of Wight: 92km

13,812km²
area

Wales: 20,779km²

HIGHEST PEAK: BOBOTOV KUK

2,522m

Ben Nevis: 1,345m

LARGEST LAKE IN THE BALKANS

LAKE SKADAR
area 370km²

Lake Geneva: 580km²

DEEPEST GORGE: TARA CANYON

>1,300m
a European record!

Grand Canyon (USA): 1,800 m

ALMOST 50 WINERIES

are spread across the country.
Most popular grape variety: Vranac

PODGORICA

Capital and also Montenegro's biggest city, with 199,700 inhabitants

117 BEACHES
MOST OF THEM PEBBLE

AVERAGE MONTHLY INCOME: 800 EUROS
UK: 2,614 euros

UNDERSTAND MONTENEGRO

DOES SIZE REALLY MATTER?

We all know that size isn't everything. However, even if this was the case, Montenegro would still be able to hold its own because looking at the population figures, the country and its 622,000 inhabitants are 168th in the world, which means that it is still ahead of Cape Verde, Kiribati and the Isle of Man!

What is particularly striking about this diminutive population is that the people here are particularly tall: Montenegrin men are the tallest in the world, and the women are beaten in height only by the Dutch. Whether this is due to the fresh mountain or sea air, the national dish of *ćevapčići* or to a longing to be closer to heaven, who knows?

CRNA GORA

During the Middle Ages, the Venetians coined the name Montenegro or "Black Mountain" when they conquered Kotor, Budva and Ulcinj. country's Slavic name is pronounced something like "Tsrna Gora". *Gora* can mean mountain and rock and also forest or wood. When the pine forests in the Durmitor Mountains are lit up by the late afternoon sunshine, the summits glimmer dark green, almost black, which is why Montenegrins call their country Crna Gora – the "Black Forest".

HEROISM & HONOUR

Čojstvo i junaštvo – honour and heroism – have always been at the top of the list of virtues in the patriarchal society of Montenegro. There are monuments celebrating heroic deeds on every corner. When the Turks controlled the Balkans, they were unable to subject the people living in the mountainous north – and so the legend of the untamed mountain princes was born. Even today, each Montenegrin man knows which clan *(pleme)* and which brotherhood *(bratsvo)* he belongs to. One of the largest clans, the Kuči, lives in Medun, near Podgorica, and even has a museum devoted to it.

WOMEN

It is probably best not to bring the topic up with local people, but for most Montenegrin women life has not always been a bed of roses in this archaic, male-dominated society. In the 1960s, women were still expected to walk a few steps behind their husbands as a sign of respect.

Things are finally changing in the 21st century and young, well-educated and self-confident Montenegrin women are slowly making changes to the man's world. Although the patriarchal structures remain deeply rooted, it is increasingly common to find successful women in politics, business and society.

REAL ESTATE

Prices exploded in 2008 after a law was passed that made it possible for foreign landowners to register property under their own name. Any locals who owned property near the Adriatic sold it off to make money. Lavish villas and luxury hotels have been built on the beaches, often blocking public access to the coast. Montenegro's most beautiful beaches between Budva and Sv. Stefan have been transformed into rows of non-descript hotels. On the other hand, the influx of foreign capital gave an enormous boost to the local economy. Thankfully, though, the unrestrained building boom has waned in recent years.

Investors were quick to secure their place in the sun in Sv. Stefan

Monumental resting place for the poet prince: Njegoš Mausoleum on Mount Lovćen

EUROFIGHTER

What? Montenegro is not an EU member but still uses the euro? After migrant workers had begun to take their hard-earned Deutsche marks (DM) home to Yugoslavia in the 1960s, the then German currency became a parallel currency to the Yugoslav dinar. In 2000, Montenegro went as far as decreeing the DM as the country's sole currency. This was seen as an early sign of Montenegrin independence from Serbia, which came fully six years later. Eventually, the country introduced the euro in 2002. Although it is not included in European decision-making processes and is not allowed to print money itself (all cash must be procured from the "real" euro zone), Montenegro has acquired a stable currency, which is pretty clever, really!

NJEGOŠ, THE POET PRINCE

Prince Bishop Petar II Petrović Njegoš (1813–51) is possibly the most multi-talented personality in Montenegrin history. He died of tuberculosis at an early age, but managed to not only reform the tiny state's outdated political system with its antiquated clan structures (and by doing so brought the country closer to Europe), but also to write the most significant work in Southern Slavic literature, *The Mountain Wreath (Gorski Vjenac)*. The work remained required reading throughout the former Yugoslavia until the start of the Balkan wars. Its subject is the "heroic struggle" of his predecessor Danilo I to liberate the country from Ottoman domination through the mass execution of Montenegrins who had converted to Islam. In *The Mountain Wreath*, Njegoš wrote down for the first time many of the verses, which have their roots in popular poetry, and in so doing significantly brought forward the standardization of the written language.

Njegoš' final resting place is in a large mausoleum on Mount Lovćen, Montenegro's "Olympus", that is easily visible from the coast as well as the highlands.

PATRON SAINTS

Every Orthodox family has a patron saint, and once a year hosts a large party lasting several days to celebrate the saint's day. *Slava* has been the most important family festival since ancient times. Its origins date back to a pre-Christian Slavic religion. People spend days preparing ritual food and cleaning the house, until the priest arrives on the saint's day and gives his blessing. Then, the celebrations begin with lots of laughter, singing and dancing. Monasteries also have their patron saints. Ostrog Monastery, for example, honours St Vasilije on 12 May.

FIFTY-FIFTY

It was a tight affair: ahead of the referendum on the separation from Serbia it was decreed that there had to be a minimum turnout of 50 per cent and the winner needed at least 55 per cent of the votes. On the day there was a huge turnout of 86 per cent, but the

TRUE OR FALSE?

HOT TEMPERED

A common perception is that people in the Balkans – and men in particular – are so hot-tempered that the slightest provocation leads to an erupting volcano and to aggression. The dreadful images from the Yugoslav Wars have done nothing to dispel this image. Therefore, it is a relief to find that most people you encounter in Montenegro are positively calm and friendly, and there is little tension in the air.

APPALLING ROADS

Are roads in Montenegro only suitable for the suicidal or the adventurous? By no means: the routes along the Adriatic coast and major roads inland and in the mountains are perfectly fine, and sometimes smoother than potholed country roads in the UK. Of course, there are tight and winding routes up to monasteries or the rough track high above Lake Skadar where you feel the need to give yourself a shake when you get out of the car. Yes, there is still adventure to be found on the roads in Montenegro, but it's not unmanageable.

The Durmitor Mountains in the high north regularly get bad weather

"yes" vote for independence came in at precisely 55.49 per cent. This of course meant that the population was divided and many people wanted to remain in Serbia, the "big brother" that had provided a cosy home for decades.

After the separation, Montenegrin became the country's official language, although many citizens kept using Serbian in daily life. In the meantime, this ratio has turned into roughly 50-50, so much so that the Serbian-speaking part of the population demands increased state support because they perceive themselves as disadvantaged.

In reality, the differences between both languages are fairly subtle. For example, the Montenegrin word for river is *rijeka*, while Serbs say *reka*; the world is *svijet* and *svet* respectively; and tomorrow translates as *sjutra* and *sutra* respectively. Key expressions, such as *dobar dan* (hello) and *hvala* (thank you), are actually identical.

In the south and northeast, things are easier for the Albanian minority who make up approximately five per cent of the population; here, bilingualism is enshrined in law.

RUSSIANS

The Montenegrins have always loved *Majka Rusija* (Mother Russia), and there are historical reasons for their enthusiasm. The Russian Tsar's soldiers fought side by side with the

RAIN

Tourists hardly give the rain a thought when they bathe in dazzling sunshine on the coast from March to October, but in spring and late autumn a few wet days sneak in. However, Montenegrin rain is rather special: it does not last long but makes up for that by being all the heavier. As soon as it starts, mountain streams gush into the sea, the sky becomes dark, white-crested waves smash against the shore, there is thunder and lightning and heavy raindrops beat down on the earth. And five minutes later, it's all over. The fragrance of plants and flowers lingers, the air is sharp and clear, the sun shines again – but only for five minutes and then the spectacle begins once more. This phenomenon is particularly violent in the mountainous north of the country.

locals during the wars against the Turks in the 19th century. Today, this loyalty has been reciprocated by the Russians who have declared Montenegro to be their second homeland. There are Russian real estate agents everywhere selling properties to their countrymen. There are 10,000 Russians living in Budva alone.

The proximity of the two nations also has practical reasons: both Russia and Montenegro use the Cyrillic alphabet and, despite not yet being an EU member state, Montenegro is regarded as a bridge towards Western Europe. Even the country's NATO membership, which was heavily criticised by Moscow, has not put Russians off from living here.

WILD BEAUTY

Besides all the commercial and political developments, Montenegro is still a place for dreamers and explorers. "Wild Beauty" is the country's advertising slogan to attract tourists, and in some places you can still find unspoiled countryside. The hospitality of the 622,000 Montenegrins is legendary. "The guest is king" is the motto in Montenegro, and your hosts will welcome you with sincerity and warmth. Countless guests have been impressed by the friendly atmosphere in their holiday home – enjoying a glass of wine on the veranda in the evening with figs, olives and cheese, relaxed conversations with hosts – creating wonderful holiday memories.

EATING
SHOPPING
SPORT

Montenegro's wild mountains offer a welcome break from the beach

EATING & DRINKING

The country might be small but the variety of its culinary delights is enormous! Most of them come from Montenegro's abundant natural resources. Contented cows graze on the mountain slopes and in the valleys. Mushrooms and wild herbs, such as mint and thyme, grow beside the main highways. There are olive groves and avenues of fig trees, and vegetables out of the garden in summer.

ORGANIC PRODUCE ON THE UP

For several years, there has been a noticeable trend towards a sustainable food culture in Montenegro, and there are now a few hundred officially registered organic farmers. In the mountains everything grows naturally, and olive and fig trees have grown in the coastal region for centuries. For many years, farmers were only able to sell their locally grown products – honey, cheese, ham, jam and olive oil as well as fruit and vegetables – at markets or fairs, but this is now changing as the large supermarkets are becoming increasingly interested in that kind of produce. Local products are also offered for sale at the side of the road – not everywhere, but often at fair prices.

SEAFOOD

Almost all restaurants on the coast and many bars serve you fish – grilled *(na žaru)*, boiled *(lešo)* or in a casserole *(brodeto)*. You can also savour mussels in white wine *(mušule buzara)* or stuffed squid *(punjeni lignji)*. In the Middle Ages, the Venetians not only left architectural traces in Montenegro, but also evidence of their culinary arts. Fine Italian cuisine still influences the gastronomy of the coastal region in pasta and fish recipes.

And it's not just the sea that's fishy:

A glass of *vino* always goes well with food: Vranac is the red variety from the Balkans

the cuisine of the entire region around Lake Skadar is also influenced by the water. This is where you will find eel, carp and bleak fish on your plate – grilled, dried, boiled, smoked or pan-fried. You can also enjoy many fish specialities such as carp and trout *(pastrmka)* in the restaurants of the capital, Podgorica.

HEARTY FOOD IN THE KONOBAS

In the highland regions around Kolašin, Žabljak and Nikšić, meat takes over and the cuisine is correspondingly hearty. Everything the pastures and farms produce finds its way to the plate – high-quality natural ingredients that will appeal to fans of organic food. You should try lamb that is baked under a *sač*, a large metal or ceramic bell-shaped lid covered with ashes and live coals. The best place to enjoy this is in a traditional round wooden hut *(savardak)*. The *njeguški*

pršut (air-dried ham) and *njeguški sir* (which is similar to ricotta), come from the village of Njeguši, between Cetinje and Kotor. These delicacies are offered in small family-run *konobas* (taverns) by the roadside. They are served with a thick slice of bread that each family bakes in a wood-burning stove following its own recipe, and a glass of *medovina* (an old Slavic honey drink). You can relax and enjoy a unique view of the Lovćen Mountains. Another special treat is the fresh goat's cheese

INSIDER TIP
Goat's cheese

mladi kozji sir. The best is produced in the Kolašin region in the northeast.

ĆEVAPČIĆI – THE NATIONAL SNACK

No meal in Montenegro would be complete without bread. The *narodni hleb* is the traditional loaf: all bakeries were required to have a stock of this so-called "people's bread", which was subsidised by the state. However, the bread is somewhat bland. This is made up for by the delicious traditional turnovers *(pita)*: sheets of *jufka* pastry filled with cheese *(sirnica)*, spinach *(zeljanica)* or meat *(burek)* and accompanied by a glass of yogurt. Typical types of Balkan fast food are *ćevapčići* (spicy meat rolls served with chips and raw onions) and *pljeskavica* (hamburger). You can buy them at kiosks across the country.

VEGETARIAN FOOD

Being vegetarian isn't ideal in Montenegro, but the situation is inproving. Sometimes a salad is all you will need on a hot summer day: the *šopska salata* includes tomatoes, cucumber, onions and peppers topped with cheese made from sheep's milk. *Kupus salata* is another delicacy: shredded cabbage with black olives in a light vinaigrette made with olive oil. Other vegetarian delicacies include grilled aubergines, stuffed vine leaves and spicy mountain cheese. Along the coast and in Podgorica you can also find vegetarian restaurants.

FOR THOSE WITH A SWEET TOOTH

Those with a sweet tooth will have a hard time in Montenegro. There are no afternoon tea cakes and none of the classic pastries that are common in Western Europe. One solution can be found on the menu of the better restaurants: the *palačinke* (pancakes) brought to Montenegro by the Austrians. The classic pancakes are filled with nuts, jam or Nutella, which is known as *eurokrem* here. With some luck, you might also find apple strudel *(štrudla od jabuka)* or plum cake *(pita od šljiva)* on the menu.

Although many varieties of fruit grow in Montenegro, fruit salad *(voćna salata)* is rarely offered in restaurants. Ice cream *(sladoled)* is much more common.

Tourists who risk the baklava (puff pastry stuffed with nuts and raisins) should not overlook the glass of water served with it: it will help you swallow the sticky pastry. The various jams and marmalades that are sold at the markets and in the supermarkets are far too sweet for most tourists' taste. However, fig jam *(marmelada od smokve)* is a really tasty speciality.

DRINKS

Meals at any time of the day are accompanied by a typical mocha. If you find this too strong or bitter, ask for it to be made with milk. These days you can also get cappuccino and latte macchiato in every town.

If you like hard liquor, you should also try the local spirits. While plum brandy *šljivovica* is the favourite in the north, people on the coast prefer the Montenegrin grappa variety known as *loza* (with an alcoholic content of over 45 per cent). Both are available throughout the country and often taken with a mocha or espresso.

Now you're set: bon appétit *(prijatno)* and cheers *(živeli)*!

Today's specials

Starters

IMAM BAJELDI
Baked aubergine stuffed with tomato, garlic and onion

CRNI RIŽOT
Risotto coloured black with squid ink

KAJMAK
Fresh creamy cheese, similar to clotted cream

SIR U ULJU
Sheep's milk cheese preserved in olive oil

Vegetarian

KAČAMAK
Cheesy Montenegrin polenta, like its Italian counterpart

PAŠTROVSKI MAKARULI
Noodles made with wholewheat flour and served with olive oil and cheese preserved in brine

Meat dishes

JAGNJETINA U MLIJEKU
Lamb cooked in milk and then baked

BALŠIĆA TAVA
Strips of veal topped with a sauce of eggs, milk and cream

NJEGUŠKA ŠNICLA
Breaded pork escalope stuffed with kajmak cheese and ham

Fish dishes

PASTRMKA U KISELOM MLIJEKU
Trout in yogurt, eaten cold

BOKELJSKI BRODET
Fish stew with sprats and hake

RIBLJA JUHA
Fish soup with gilthead seabream

KRAP U TAVU
Carp cooked in a pan and served with prunes, apples and quince

Drinks

KRSTAČ
Full-bodied, dry white wine

VRANAC PRO CORDE
Dry, dark red wine

NIKŠIĆKO PIVO
The Montenegrin beer

SHOPPING

HANDMADE

The long winter evenings in the mountains in the north are the time for wood carving, knitting and crocheting. In former times, the mountain villages were snowed in from December to March, and traditional handicrafts helped people pass the time and provided useful items for the clan. Today, hand-crafted goods are still produced – for the tourists. The arts and crafts are sold outside the house, where large bowls decorated with floral motifs or simple boards and cutlery of all sizes await their buyers. Wooden articles are offered at the markets and in the souvenir shops (avoid those made of teak – they are cheap imports).

The wool pullovers might not be haute couture, but they are cosy – and sometimes a bit scratchy (because the wool has not been treated with any chemicals. Authentic hand-embroidered blouses and dresses and crocheted tablecloths are becoming increasingly difficult to find.

JEWELLERY

If you are interested in the filigree works of the local silversmiths, you will find any number of inexpensive silver necklaces, rings and bracelets in Ulcinj on the Albanian border. Many of the jewellery shops are located on *Ulica zlatara* – the name is somewhat confusing as it means "street of the goldsmiths".

BARGAINING FOR THE FUN OF IT

A visit to a market in Montenegro is a special experience; most are held from the morning to the early afternoon. The farmers' markets in the cities – and particularly in Bar – are a real treat: fragrant, colourful local produce in all its splendour lies spread out on wooden tables. Playful bargaining for a few cents or euros may

Markets offer wool clothing for those cold winter days (left)

bring a smile to your and the sellers' faces.

Each village also has a market where all kinds of other goods – inexpensive clothing (but watch out for fake designer brands!), hats made of fabric and leather, brooches with shells and wooden beer mugs – are sold. Sometimes a farmers' market is included and it is usually cheerful, loud and inexpensive. Every visitor to Montenegro should experience these markets at least once. One of the most beautiful is in Tuzi, a small village between Podgorica and the Albanian border.

INSIDER TIP
Experience
the spectacle

HANDMADE IN THE MONASTERY

You will not only be able to purchase pictures of Orthodox saints at the various markets but also in the souvenir shops at monasteries. These icons do not cost very much, but they mean a lot to the people. Various other products for sale in the monastery shops include honey, creams and ointments made by the nuns or monks – all 100% plant-based and good for you!

FASHION IN MONTENEGRO

There is a wide choice of fashion shops in Montenegro. There are elegant glass and marble boutiques selling exclusive brands, such as Prada and Jil Sander, and Italian shoes in chic Porto Montenegro. And at the markets you can buy breezy cotton summer dresses for a mere 10 or 20 euros. Local designer clothing is sold in the fashion boutiques in the old towns of Budva, Kotor, Herceg Novi and Podgorica; many of the pieces have been inspired by traditional costumes and based on old patterns – long dresses with wide sleeves – or decorated with ornaments made with silver or gold threads.

SPORT & ACTIVITIES

From angling to windsurfing, Montenegro offers everything a sporting enthusiast's heart desires. It is possible to ski in some mountain valleys until July, while hikers can explore the north of the country on snow-free trails from April. The infrastructure in the Bjelasica, Prokletije, Durmitor and Lovćen mountain regions, as well as around Lake Skadar, has greatly improved in recent years, and tourists are now offered a choice between alpine huts, camping sites and sports clubs. On the Adriatic coast visitors can relax outside in the balmy spring air from April, and diving is not a problem – if you have a wetsuit. The Adriatic has an average temperature of over 20°C until well into October, providing ideal conditions for water sports such as snorkelling, swimming and sailing.

CANOEING & RAFTING

The windy Bay of Kotor is great fun for canoeing and kayaking because, although you are in salt water, it feels more like gliding across a calm lake. The bay offers spectacular views, for example of Baroque Perast and the church island of Gospa od Škrpjela. Lake Skadar is rather the opposite: an ocean feeling on a freshwater lake; but it's just as nice for paddling.

A rafting tour on the Tara River is one of the highlights of any holiday in Montenegro. The river carves its way for more than 100km through the highlands in the northwest – and provides lots of thrills and spills for the rafters. Tackling the frothing waves in the deep canyon is an unforgettable experience. Operators in Kolašin and Žabljak organise rafting tours of various lengths on both the Tara River and on

INSIDER TIP Rafting on wild rivers

Whitewater rafting on the River Tara

the Piva River that joins the Tara at the border with Bosnia-Herzegovina. Two operators from Kolašin provide trips throughout the north of the country with exceptionally well-trained guides: *Explorer (Mojkovačka | mobile 067 26 31 38 | explorer.co.me)* and *Eco-Tours (Dunje Đokić | mobile 067 25 90 20 | eco-tours.co.me)*.

FISHING

Dozens of rivers and hundreds of streams plus countless lakes and, of course, the Adriatic Sea: Montenegro is a dream for fishermen. One of the best operators of fishing tours is *Kingfisher (mobile 067 01 90 95 | skadarlakeboatcruise.com)* in Virpazar on Lake Skadar. The choice is greatest along the Adriatic coast, but in the uplands the Crno jezero (Black Lake) near Žabljak as well as the rivers Morača and Lim are home to numerous species of fish.

KITESURFING & PARAGLIDING

Along the coast, Budva and Ada Bojana are popular spots for paragliders and kitesurfers. Strong winds and long beaches make for ideal conditions to get airborne. But these activities are also possible on beaches between Tivat and Ulcinj. *Paragliding Montenegro (mobile 069 02 23 52 | paraglidingmontenegro.com)* offers information for paragliders. In the north, Berane is developing as a centre for the sport.

MOUNTAIN BIKING & HIKING

An increasing number of visitors are leaving the beaches and getting out their hiking boots and bicycles to explore new territory far away from the coast. A nationwide network of cycle and hiking paths of around 6,000km has been established within the framework of the *Wilderness Hiking & Biking* project in an effort to integrate the hinterland into the country's tourist activities. Almost all of the trails lead into the fascinating landscape of the north – where there are over 150 mountains that are more than 2,000m high. Most of the hikes are well signposted. Cyclists can choose between six national trails, ranging from easy-going to demanding, in addition to other local routes. Renting a bike can be difficult, especially if operators do not have enough bikes on hand. Ask at the local tourist office for more information.

Be cautious in the wild north of the country and remember that your safety should always come first (see p. 144). It is recommended you take a guide who knows the area. In an emergency you can get help from the mountain rescue service *(Gorska sluzba spasavanja Crne Gore | gss-cg. me/english | tel. 040 25 60 84)* or the police *(tel. 122).*

SAILING

There are some well-equipped marinas between Herceg Novi and Bar for Adriatic yachtsmen. The *Porto Montenegro (portomontenegro.com)* operation in Tivat aims to outdo Monaco and Saint Tropez. The countless regattas – mainly for small and medium-mast boats – show just how important this sport is in Montenegro. You can charter yachts and motorboats in any of the larger towns on the coast. Podgorica is also the headquarters of the *Montenegro Charter Company (Bulevar Sv. Petra Cetinjskog 92 | mobile 067 20 16 55 | monte negrocharter.com).*

There are wonderful fishing spots on the coast and in the many lakes and rivers

SCUBA DIVING

Pleasant water temperatures and interesting dive sites such as coral reefs, sunken ships and underwater caves make the Montenegrin Adriatic ideal for divers. The water along the coast is around 35m deep and the summer sea temperatures are between 21°C and 25°C. The dive certificates issued by the established international organisations are recognised, however, it is only possible to dive with Montenegrin companies.

The international database *divecenters.net* offers a good overview of the local enterprises – enter "Montenegro" in the search field on the homepage.

SKIING

Thanks to the exceptional infrastructure, empty slopes and reasonable prices (day pass from approx. 20 euros; skiing equipment approx. 20 euros per day), Montenegro is a popular destination for winter sports fans. The continental climate in the north guarantees freezing winters with plenty of snow in the Montenegrin mountains even in these times of climate change. The season lasts from December to April. Durmitor near Žabljak and Bjelasica near Kolašin are the best known of Montenegro's numerous skiing regions with slopes up to 2,000m.

STAND-UP PADDLING (SUP)

Now this trendy sport has reached Montenegro as well, which is great because conditions in many spots are just fabulous, especially in the protected Bay of Kotor but also in Budva further south. One of several excellent operators in Kotor is the *SUP Montenegro* adventure and sports centre *(tel. 069 19 01 90 | supmontenegro.me).*

TENNIS

Novak Đoković is for Montenegro what Andy Murray is for the UK. Although the international tennis star is Serbian, his family comes from the country of the black mountains – this is why he is celebrated here as "our Novak". The Canadian-born Milos Raonic, from Podgorica, who has been a leading player in the world for many years, is also regarded as "one of us". The Montenegrins' love of tennis makes the tennis association *Teniski Savez Crne Gore (mta.co.me)* popular. This also benefits tourists, as many coastal resorts now have tennis courts, for example, in Herceg Novi, Tivat, Budva, Bar or Ada Bojana. Tennis courts are also found inland, e.g. in Podgorica, Berane or Nikšić. You will find the addresses at local tourist offices, but registration is necessary.

WINDSURFING

Experienced windsurfers will be delighted by the high waves and strong winds off the coast near Ulcinj. Beginners, on the other hand, should stay in the protected waters of the Bay of Kotor. It is also fun to try the freshwater variety: people have recently started windsurfing on Lake Skadar once again.

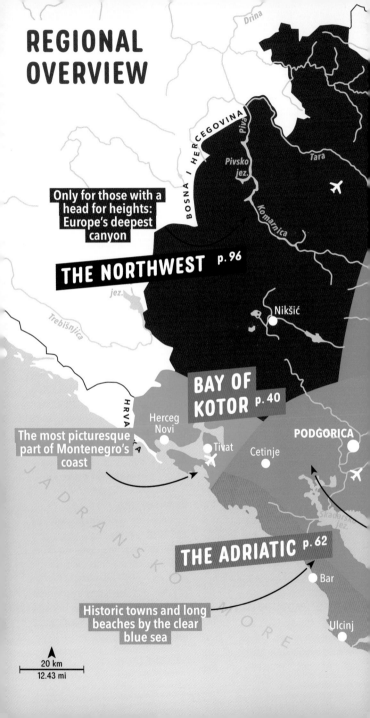

REGIONAL OVERVIEW

Only for those with a head for heights: Europe's deepest canyon

THE NORTHWEST p. 96

Nikšić

BAY OF KOTOR p. 40

The most picturesque part of Montenegro's coast

Herceg Novi

PODGORICA

Tivat

Cetinje

THE ADRIATIC p. 62

Bar

Historic towns and long beaches by the clear blue sea

Ulcinj

BOSNA I HERCEGOVINA

Drina

Piva

Tara

Pivsko jez.

Komarnica

jez.

Trebišnjica

HRVA...A

J A D R A N S K O   M O R E

Skada... jez.

20 km
12.43 mi

ievlja

SRBIJA

Zlatarsko
jezero

Uvac

Ibar

THE NORTHEAST p. 108

Real skiing and hiking adventures in the wild mountains

Bijelo Polje

ojkovac

Berane

Gazivode
jez.

Kolašin

CRNA GORA

Lim

KOSOVË

SHQIPËRIA (ALBANIA)

CETINJE, SKUTARISEE & PODGORICA p. 80

Old capital, new capital and the most important lake in the Balkans

Drin

Drin

ueni

Liqeni i Vaut
të Dejeës

BAY OF KOTOR

HEAVENLY BLUE

Regardless of whether you catch the first glimpse from the air or after driving the serpentine road down to Kotor from Montenegro's own Olympus, the Lovćen: nowhere else in Montenegro do steep rock faces and the glittering green Adriatic meet as harmoniously as they do in the spectacular natural setting of the Bay of Kotor *(Boka Kotorska).*

There are also man-made masterpieces here: seen from above, the small church islands off the coast of Perast, Sv. Đorđe and Gospa

The church island of Gospa od Škrpjela is located in the deep, wide bay

od Škrpjela (Our Lady of the Rocks), shine in the water like pebbles in a pool. Framed by the Orjen Mountains in the west and the Lovćen in the east, the bay attracted ruling families and sailors from early times.

The 70km-long coastal road winds its way past palm trees, small beaches and charming old stone houses from Herceg Novi to Tivat which, along with Kotor, are the largest cities on the bay. Lord Byron visited the Bay of Kotor in 1809 and wrote: "When the pearls of nature were sown, handfuls of them were cast on this soil."

BAY OF KOTOR

KOTOR

Morinj

M12

Kameno

HERCEG NOVI

CRNA GORA / ЦРНА ГОРА

Trebesin

Sasovići

Sušćepan

Podi

1 Igalo M1

45km, 1 hr

Zelenika

Bijela **3**

Herceg Novi ★
p. 44

2 Savina

M1

Kumbor

Baošići

Provodina

Hercegnovski zaliv

☀
⛱
Đenovići

Kumburski tjesnac

20km, 1 hr

Boka kotorska

HERCEG NOVI

Krašić

☀
⛱
Plaža Arza

12 **Luštica**

J A D R A N S K O   M O R E

↑
2 km
1.24 mi

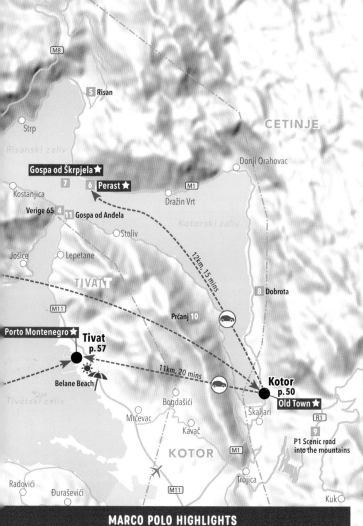

Strp

M8

5 Risan

CETINJE

Donji Orahovac

Risanski zaliv

Gospa od Škrpjela★

7 6 **Perast ★**

Kostanjica

Verige 65 4 11 Gospa od Anđela

Dražin Vrt

M1

Kotorski zaliv

Stoliv

Jošice

Lepetane

TIVAT

M11

12km, 15 mins

8 Dobrota

Porto Montenegro ★

Tivat
p. 57

Prčanj 10

Belane Beach

11km, 20 mins

Tivatski zaliv

Bogdašići

Mrčevac

Kavač

Kotor
p. 50

Old Town ★

Škaljari

R1

KOTOR

M1

P1 Scenic road
into the mountains

Radovići

Đuraševići

M11

Trojica

Kuk

MARCO POLO HIGHLIGHTS

★ **HERCEG NOVI**
Every year, the first place to feel spring in
Montenegro is the lovely "flower town" at the
entrance to the Bay of Kotor ➤ p. 44

★ **KOTOR OLD TOWN**
The architectural monuments behind Kotor's
thick city walls recall centuries of fascinating
history ➤ p. 51

★ **PERAST**
The sleepy little town takes visitors back to a
bygone era when illustrious captains put out
to sea from here ➤ p. 54

★ **GOSPA OD ŠKRPJELA**
Built on top of shipwrecks and boulders,
the Church of Our Lady of the Rocks, with
its magnificent Baroque interior, perches in
splendour off the coast of Perast ➤ p. 54

★ **PORTO MONTENEGRO**
Today, superyachts bob up and down in the
luxury marina that was once the naval base
of Tivat ➤ p. 58

★ **LUŠTICA**
Pristine bays, olive groves and deserted villages
– the peninsula is a tranquil paradise. ➤ p. 60

HERCEG NOVI

(📖 H5) **The Yugoslavian Nobel Prize laureate Ivo Andrić described ⭐ Herceg Novi (pop. 14,000) as the city of "eternal greenery, sun and promenades".**

When the north of Montenegro is still in the grip of icy winter tempera-

plants with them when they returned from their voyages and, paired with the flora of the Mediterranean region, they blossom in colourful splendour every spring.

The mix of architectural styles from Oriental to Baroque lends Herceg Novi – which is situated on a steep escarpment with long flights of steps – a touch of elegance that always

After you've climbed the "100,000 steps", you can sit back and relax in an old town café

tures, the first flowers start to bloom in the harbour town that was founded in 1382 by the Bosnian King Tvrtko I and later named after Duke *(Herceg)* Stijepan Vukšić. This is celebrated every year with a feast of wine and fresh fish held in late January/early February when thousands of people throng the waterfront promenade *(obala)* for the Mimosa Festival. The city's famous seafarers brought exotic

charms its visitors. The "City of 100,000 Steps" once again became the favourite holiday destination for Belgrade's artistic elite after the end of the Balkan wars. They were particularly attracted by the town's lively cultural life.

The 7km-long promenade *Šetalište Pet Danica* stretches from the spa town of Igalo to Meljine and is lined with cafés, restaurant and jetties. This is the place to see and be seen – with mirrored sunglasses, the latest smartphones and chic designer outfits. The Obala forms the heart of the Herceg Nova Riviera that stretches from *Njivice* to *Kamenari*: the landmark mountain *Orjen* (1,893m) dominates the background, the sun rises over the Prevlaka Peninsula and sets behind the Mamula fortress island, and there are especially wonderful views of all of this from the Obala.

Many sights on the beautiful Luštica Peninsula (see p. 60) are easy to reach from Herceg Novi. If you want to get from Tivat to Herceg Novi quickly, take the car ferry from Kamenari (15km east of Herceg Novi) to Lepetane (5km north of Tivat) *(operating around the clock, non-stop during the day | cars 4.50 euros, pedestrians free | ferry.co.me).*

SIGHTSEEING

OLD TOWN (STARI GRAD)
A flight of steps leads from *Nikole Đurković Square*, the city's bustling meeting place, with cafés and shops, in the centre of town, through Herceg Novi's most famous landmark, the clock tower *(Sahat kula),* commissioned by Sultan Mahmud in 1667. The Orthodox Archangel Michael Church *(Sv. Arhanđela Mihaila),* with its Romanesque, Gothic and Oriental elements, lies behind the clock tower on pretty, palm tree-fringed *Herceg Stjepan Square*. The city's *archives* take up the northern end of the square and there is a *library* with 30,000 volumes

on the south side.

Follow the narrow streets down through the old town and you will land right in front of the entrance to the *Forte Mare*. The fortified tower was constructed between the 14th and 17th centuries and today films are shown here on a big screen in the summer.

GALERIE JOSIP BEPO BENKOVIĆ

One of the oldest galleries in the country exhibits modern art by young talents from Serbia and Montenegro. New works are presented and awarded prizes at a winter salon in February, which has been organised by the gallery since 1966. *May–Sept daily 9am–11pm, Oct–April 9am–5pm | Marka Vojnovića 4 | short. travel/mon7 | admission free | ⏱ 1 hr*

KANLI KULA
The fortress, whose name translates as "bloody tower" and which was constructed at the upper end of the old town during the Turkish period, served as a bastion and prison for many years. With seating for more than 1,000, it is now one of the most beautiful open-air stages on the Adriatic. And the views of the bay are fantastic! You absolutely must try to get tickets for one of the concerts. *Daily 9am–7pm | admission 2 euros | ⏱ 2 hrs incl. walking there and back*

TVRĐAVA ŠPANJOLA
Construction of this Spanish fortress, which towers over the city and offers visitors a magnificent view of the bay

and Prevlaka Peninsula, was started by the Spaniards in 1538 and later completed by the Turks. Enjoy the incredible views of the bay and the Prevlaka Peninsula. The fortress is open around the clock, which means that you can admire the stunning Adriatic at dusk! *Admission free | ⏱ 2 hrs incl. the walk there and back from the old town*

INSIDER TIP
Night-time views

ZAVIČAJNI MUZEJ

Archaeological finds from the early days of Herceg Novi – when Illyrians, Greeks and Romans settled in the area – are displayed on the two floors of the well-presented Regional Museum. *Tue–Sun 8am–7pm | Mirka Komnenovića 9 | short.travel/mon8 | admission 3 euros | ⏱ 1 hr*

EATING & DRINKING

Many pizzerias and restaurants serving grilled meat and fish line the *Šetalište Pet Danica*. And most of the city's beaches are turned into bars, pubs and discotheques in the evening.

GRADSKA KAFANA – RESTORAN TERASA DI PALMA

The *Gradska Kafana*, or town café, is the spot where locals like to spend their time enjoying an espresso or generous meal. This café is becoming increasingly popular with tourists too. The cuisine is international, and the view from the three terraces over the bay and old town is unforgettable. *Njegoševa 31 | tel. 031 32 40 67 | gradskakafana.me | €€*

PETER'S PIE & COFFEE

Who said that you can't eat healthily in Montenegro? Here they serve vegetarian, vegan and many other delicacies. Plus, there's excellent coffee and tea in a prime location at the promenade with marvellous views. Friendly, English-speaking staff. Diabetics and health-conscious guests can enjoy sugar-free cake and other desserts. *Šetalište Pet Danica 18a | mobile 067 14 81 80 | €€*

INSIDER TIP
Sweet, but not sugary

TRI LIPE

There is no better place to eat in Herceg Novi: this restaurant close to the harbour – named after the three lime trees that provide wonderful shade – serves great grilled skewers and other classics of Balkan cuisine. Cosy atmosphere, fair prices and attentive staff. *Stepenište 28 | tel. 031 32 11 07 | €€*

SHOPPING

KNJIŽARA SO

The bookstore's name (*So* means salt) is a reminder that Herceg Novi was established in the wake of the salt trade. It is located on the former "Salt Square" where the white gold was traded in times gone by. There is a wide selection of books in many languages and the staff speak English. Browse your newly purchased books over a cup of coffee at one of the bars on the square. *Trg Nikole Đurkovića 3 | knjizaraso.com*

SPORT & ACTIVITIES

BARKARIOLI

The Italian word *barca* (boat) inspired the name of the local association of operators who offer boat excursions for tourists in Herceg Novi. The 25 boats ferry passengers for reasonable prices to the beaches and towns on the Bay of Kotor. A *barca* is always available round-the-clock. *Topla 3 | at the harbour | mobile 067 30 09 43*

GORBIS TRAVEL

The travel agents not only organise private accommodation but also boat tours of the Bay of Kotor and day trips to Ostrog Monastery near Nikšić, as well as to Dubrovnik and Lake Skadar. *Njegoševa 66 | tel. 031 32 44 23 | gorbis.com*

TENISKI CENTAR SBS

In spring and autumn this is the site of two Grand Slam tournaments. Court fees from 10 euros/hr; lessons as well as floodlit courts available. *Šetalište Pet Danica 8a | tel. 031 32 40 40*

BEACHES

The large hotels have man-made beaches (i.e. concrete platforms) and there is a lovely sandy beach *(Blatna plaža)* at the western end of the pedestrian promenade below the Igalo Institute.

Those who prefer to swim further away from town should take the small coastal road towards Bijela where the beaches in *Zelenika*, *Kumbor* and *Balošići* are not as crowded as those in Herceg Novi. *Đenovići Beach (8km from Kotor)* with its imported sand and sun loungers in a relaxed hamlet is particularly enjoyable, offering several small restaurants and cafés as well as a small marina and chic promenade.

Holidaying in Herceg Novi means bathing with a historic backdrop

Boats leave the harbour for *Njivice* (*H6*), where the nudist beach of the Hotel Riviera is also open to non-guests. Herceg Novi's most beautiful beaches are on the *Luštica Peninsula*, on the other side of the bay, and can be easily reached by boat. One thing applies here and for all the other beaches in the Bay of Kotor: as there is hardly any inflow from the sea, the water sometimes becomes a little stagnant.

FESTIVALS

INTERNATIONAL CHILDREN'S CARNIVAL 👶

Every June, groups from the whole of Montenegro and abroad gather to celebrate a colourful street carnival. Whether infants or adolescents, all are united in the pure joy of dressing up, dancing, singing and parading. The children symbolically take over the "control of the town". *1st weekend in June | hercegnovi.me*

NIGHTLIFE

The promenade along the shore stretches for about a mile and is lined with countless bars, cafés, pubs and restaurants. When the heat of the day gives way to the cool of the evening, young and old flock to the beach for fun into the early hours: at the *Bolivar (local bands)*, *Casa Igalo (house and techno | FB)*, *Nautica (jazz)* and *Copas (with sun loungers right on the beach | open 24/7 | FB: copashercegnovi).*

AROUND HERCEG NOVI

1 IGALO

4km west of Herceg Novi, 5 mins by car on the E65

The spa town (pop. 3,000) is situated at the west end of the promenade, only a 15-minute walk from the harbour of Herceg Novi. Rheumatics have long appreciated the beneficial effects of the minerals in the mud from the shallow sea, and the first health centre was built here in 1950. Today, the spa and wellness facilities at the *Institut Igalo* or *Mediterranean Health Center (Save Ilica 1 | tel. 031 65 85 55 | igalo spa.com)* match Western European standards, though at more reasonable prices. Adjacent to the Institut Igalo is the *Villa Galeb (Sava Ilića 5 | tel. 031 65 85 55 | admission 3 euros | ⏱ 30 mins)*. The majestic, luxury villa was commissioned as a summer residence by the former Yugoslavian president Tito during the 1960s. The villa is rarely open and, if it is, opening hours vary. *H5*

2 SAVINA

2km east of Herceg Novi, 20 mins on foot on local roads

The small village (pop. 1,000) set in lush greenery is only a short walk from the harbour in Herceg Novi. The *Orthodox monastery (daily 7am–7pm)* with its two churches a little bit above the waterfront promenade has in its treasury the almost 800-year-old Bishop's Cross of Saint Sava, the

It may be hard to believe, but the views are not the main highlight at Savina Monastery

patron saint of the Serbian Orthodox Church. The monastery is one of the country's most beautiful and is worth seeing for its iconostasis alone, but the views of the coast are equally breathtaking. *H5*

▐3▐ BIJELA ☂

12km east of Herceg Novi, 10 mins by car on the E65

This community (pop. 4,000) is the ideal place for divers and other water-sports enthusiasts to spend their Boka holiday. The *Hotel Delfin* (tel. 031 68 34 00 | hotel-delfin.me) has a gym as well as facilities for boxing, judo, tennis, football and basketball. The Regional Center for Divers Training (tel. 031 68 34 77 | rcud.me) organises courses for beginners and advanced divers. In *Morinj*, 8km towards Kotor, you can dine elegantly

SIDER TIP
Scuba diving galore

in the atmospheric old mill *Čatovića Mlini (tel. 032 37 30 30 | catovica-mlini.com | €€€)*. It has been considered one of the best restaurants in the country for many years and serves excellent cuisine, especially fish, in its splendid gardens. Booking is essential during high season. *J5*

▐4▐ VERIGE 65

17km east of Herceg Novi, 30 mins on the E65 coastal road

At the promontory shortly after the ferry to Tivat the bay visibly widens, and you get a fabulous panorama across the water to the opposite shore with the historic town of Perast as well as the charming small islands of Gospa od Škrpjela and Sv. Đorđe. The car park at the viewpoint belongs to the stylish and modern *Verige 65* restaurant where they serve everything from traditional cuisine to sushi. The desserts are equally delicious.

However, you are welcome to just sit down with a drink and enjoy this very special spot. The car park is quite big so even non-guests can take their time to capture some exceptional shots of the bay. *Kostanjica 19, E65 | tel. 067 65 65 75 | verige65.com | €€–€€€ | ⫘ J5*

KOTOR

(⫘ K5) **Wake up in the morning to the sound of bells chiming – there are almost a dozen churches in the historic old town of Kotor (pop. 6,000). The area was declared a UNESCO World Heritage Site after the earthquake in 1979 to ensure that it was reconstructed without delay.**

Every day, the people living in Kotor can enjoy the reconstructed old town when they relax in one of the cafés on the square – polished smooth by countless footsteps – in front of the clock tower. This is probably the best place to get a feeling for the spirit of the city that was in the past ruled by the Romans, Venetians and Austrians.

In the Middle Ages the small town at the southeast corner of the bay was dominated by the Venetians. It is home to the Cathedral of Saint Tryphon, built in 1166 on the foundations of a ninth-century church. Kotor's ancient walls reflect the strength of the independent seafaring community that managed to withstand the invasion of the Turks. It was once named Dekadron and then Catarum, Catera and Cathara by a series of rulers. The name of Kotor prevailed among the South Slavs, and is a fitting name indeed because *kot* means cat in Montenegrin – and there are hundreds and hundreds of them in the town.

A string of picturesque villages along the coast towards Herceg Novi all have magnificent views of the bay and are within easy reach by bus. The narrow strait of the Adriatic attracts numerous cruise ships and excursion boats which bring not just day trippers but sadly exhaust fumes as well.

In the thick of things: the clock tower square in Kotor's old town

SIGHTSEEING

OLD TOWN (STARI GRAD) ★ ⚑

Visiting Kotor's old town is like going back in time. Three gates lead into the historic Stari grad; the oldest is the one in the south that was built as early as the 13th century. The northern gate and the main gate *(Morska vrata)* in front of the large car park on the shore – the old town is a pedestrian zone – were built in the Renaissance style in the 16th century. The *clock tower (Sat kula)* is opposite the main gate with the palaces of the patrician Bisanti and Beskuca families in the background. In addition to the *St Luka* *Church*, which was shared by Catholic and Orthodox worshippers until well into the 19th century, the *St Tryphon's Cathedral* is especially worth visiting. It suffered severe damage in the 1979 earthquake but has since been completely restored.

POMORSKI MUZEJ ☂

The three floors of the former palace of the Grgurina family houses Kotor's Maritime Museum. There is an exhibition of sailors' clothing, models of old ships, typical weapons and a relief map of the bay. An audio guide provides interesting facts. *July, Aug Mon–Sat 8am–11pm, Sun 10am–4pm;*

No pain, no gain: the ascent to Kotor's fortress is not for the faint-hearted

another entry point behind the clock tower. You need to be in good shape to climb the 1,350 well-worn steps to the *Sv. Ivan* fortress. In addition, you need to give way to oncoming "traffic". However, the views from the top are second to none and will reward you for your hard work. Please don't try the ascent in the midday heat! *Admission 8 euros*

INSIDER TIP
Keep a cool head!

JEWISH CEMETERY
The Jewish people who came to Montenegro from the Iberian Peninsula in the Middle Ages were known as "Spanish Jews". The country's new Jewish community, which was only established in 2011, has not been able to find any written documents on Jewish life in the country in medieval times, but the cemetery in Kotor provides sufficient proof that Jewish people have lived here for centuries. The site – the only Jewish cemetery in Montenegro and one of the few in the Balkans – was restored in 2005. *Škaljari district*

EATING & DRINKING

BASTION
The restaurant at the northern entrance to the old town offers a splendid range of fresh fish. Try the squid stuffed with ham and cheese. They have two other branches at *Bastion 2* and *Bastion 3*. *Trg od drva | tel. 032 32 21 16 | bastion123.com | €€*

otherwise Mon-Sat 8am-6pm, Sun 9am-1pm; in winter Mon-Fri 9am-5pm, Sat/Sun 9am-noon | Trg Bokeljske mornarice 391 | museum maritimum.com | admission 4 euros | ⊙ 1 hr

CITY WALLS & FORTRESS
The most scenic fitness training in the whole of Montenegro: begun in 1420 by the Venetians, the *city walls*, which cut deeply into the mountain above Kotor, were not completed until 400 years later. The walls stretch for more than 4km and the ascent begins shortly after the north gate, with

BBQ TANJGA

Street food is often the best, and here you get simple but delicious grilled food with a tasty marinade to take away or eat in. Choose your piece of meat, which is then freshly prepared for you. The owner speaks good English. *Šuranj bb | on the E65 near the big roundabout | €*

NSIDER TIP
Which steak do you fancy?

GALION

Enjoy the exquisite cuisine of this restaurant right on the waterfront overlooking the old town and choose between 130 imported and local wines. The ambience is exquisite, too. *Šuranj bb | tel. 032 32 50 54 | galion. me | €€€*

KONOBA CESARICA

Dalmatian fish specialities, but also sheep's milk cheese from local farmers and T-bone steaks are on the menu. Friendly service and reasonable prices in a charming atmosphere. *Stari grad 375 | tel. 032 33 60 93 | FB: Cesarica Kotor | €€*

MARSHALL'S GELATO

The opinions are unanimous: Marshall's home-made ice cream is simply fantastic! The fact that certain varieties such as tahini, salty pistachio, blueberry and cardamom require some explanation by the staff only serves to increase expectations. Not entirely cheap, but worth every cent. *In the old town near Bokeljske Mornarice Square | Stari grad bb | marshallsgelato.com*

SPORT & ACTIVITIES

KAYAKING TOURS

At *Kotor Bay Tours (Dobrota | Donji Put 255 | tel. 069 25 56 27 | kotorbay tours.com)* you can hire a kayak and go paddling. They also offer well-organised tours to the historic islands and harbours.

NIGHTLIFE

The *Jazz Club Evergreen (on Pjaci od Muzeja Square | FB: Jazz Club Evergreen)* in the centre of the old town is ideal for finishing your perfect day in Kotor with regular live jazz and blues music and great drinks.

Perfect for a quiet atmosphere is the *Old Winery Bar (Zanatska 483)* in the old town.

AROUND KOTOR

5 RISAN

18km from Kotor, 20 mins by car on the E80 and E65

The Illyrian Queen Teuta established her residence in the oldest town on the bay (pop. 1,000) in the third century BCE before it was taken by the Romans about 100 years later. The floor mosaics from the Roman period, when Risan was the most important town in the region, can be seen in an *open-air museum (Mon–Fri 8am–4pm, Sat/Sun 10am–4pm | admission 6 euros | ⏱ 30 mins)* a short way above the filling station. *J4*

6 PERAST ★

12km from Kotor, 15 mins by car on the E80 and E65

Don't miss Perast. It is one of the most beautiful small Baroque towns on the Adriatic, with a centre that is entirely listed. This attractive town boasts the most hours of sunshine per day in the country. The busts in front of the 15th-century Baroque *Sv. Nikola* church, with its 55m-high bell tower, indicate what the town is famous for: its captains, who taught Tsar Peter the Great's sailors all they knew. Today, only 300 people live in the village but at one time the fleet of this community (that was declared autonomous in 1558) was larger than that of Dubrovnik.

Under Venetian rule for centuries, Perast was repeatedly attacked by the ships of the Ottoman Empire but they were never able to take the city. Its status as an important border town gave its inhabitants many privileges that ended abruptly with the fall of Venice in 1797 and led to the downfall of the proud fraternity of seamen. The *museum of Perast (Muzej grada Perasta | daily 9am–6pm | on the shore | muzejperast.me | admission 5 euros | ⏱ 1 hr)* is located in the 17th-century *Bujović Palace*. Portraits of the city's illustrious captains, maps and the furnishings of the Bujović family make it possible for visitors to immerse themselves in the bygone world of the seafarers.

INSIDER TIP
Seafood with a sea view

The Hotel-Restaurant Conte in a dream location and with a chic terrace was also a captain's house at one time. The restaurant is right on the seafront and you simply must try the grilled scampi *(Marka Martinovića bb | tel. 032 37 36 87 | hotelconte.me | €€€)*.

Irrespective of the direction you are coming from, cars are not allowed in the centre, but have to be parked on the edge of town. Here, somewhat pushy, albeit humorous men will try to sell you boat tours and other stuff you may or may not want, and it's best to ignore their advances. However, the car park fee of 3 euros will need to be paid regardless. ⬚ J4

7 GOSPA OD ŠKRPJELA ★

15km from Kotor, 15 mins by car plus a 5-min ride by taxi ferry from Perast

One of the highlights of any Boka trip is a visit to the two church islands off the coast near Perast. The original Gospa od Škrpjela (Our Lady of the Rocks) was built in 1452. Every year, boats sail across on 22 July to celebrate the anniversary by throwing stones into the water around the island. This custom has a long tradition: for decades, sailors and fishermen sunk boats and piled up boulders on what was originally the small area of the rock until, in the middle of the 17th century, there was enough space to expand the church and add some new buildings. The house of worship was given its Baroque interior by the architect Ilija Katičić who added the bell tower and improved the nave of the church.

The hundreds of votive pictures in the church showing ships and scenes of everyday life in Perast are tokens of appreciation for being miraculously cured of a disease.

The island *Sv. Đorđe* (Saint George), opposite Gospa od Škrpjela, was for a long period the most important Benedictine abbey in the bay. In contrast to its sister church, Sv. Đorđe dominates the scene from atop a natural stone reef. Boat tours can be booked in all the towns and villages along the coast. *J4*

8 DOBROTA

4km from Kotor, 5 mins by car on the E80 and E65

This suburb of Kotor (pop. 7,000) has many small beaches and stretches for more than 7km along the coast. The

Ellas Restaurant (Dobrota 85 | mobile 069 22 04 55 | restoranelas.com | €€) on the waterfront offers something a little different as it specialises in Greek food. Delicious food is also served at the *Konoba Portun (Donji put 168 | mobile 068 08 61 01 | FB: Konoba Portun1 | €€)* which has an equally charming location by the waterside and offers exquisite fish and seafood. *K4–5*

9 P1 SCENIC ROAD INTO THE MOUNTAINS

40km, driving time (without stops) from Kotor to the viewpoint and back 1½ hrs

Starting in Kotor, initially take the P22

The sumptuous interior of Gospa od Škrpjela church

southbound, which also leads to Budva. After Škaljari village, turn left onto the mountain road. Looking at the map, the P1 which begins here looks pretty daunting with its tight bends. In reality, despite being windy and steep, the road can be managed quite well provided you pay attention and take the necessary care. Although it isn't always wide enough for two cars to pass each other, there are numerous passing places, and up until now no driver has ever had to reverse all the way back to Kotor ….

En route there is no single point from where you can admire the Bay of Kotor far below you. Instead, the entire route is scenic, with spectacular views as you climb higher and higher. One viewpoint *(GPS coordinates: 42.399398, 18.783495)* allows you almost bird's-eye views of the bay. Also visible is the Bay of Tivat with the big airport. On your return to Kotor there are many other, equally marvellous views. Another option is to continue on the P1 – in parts on a brand-new, wide section – towards Njegoš Mausoleum and Cetinje (see p. 84). □ K5

⑩ PRČANJ

5km from Kotor, 5 mins by car on the Jadranska magistrala road

Long ago this small town (pop. 1,000) played a decisive role when its seamen established the first postal service between Venice and Constantinople in the 17th century. There is a monument to Prčanj's most famous captain, Ivo Visin, in front of the parish church *Bogordični hram*, the largest in the Boka.

The steep ascent on the P1 will reward you with spectacular views of the bay

Centuries-old buildings, the idyllic harbour panorama and the relaxed atmosphere of this quiet place provide a nice contrast to busy Kotor.

Delicious fish is served in the *Restoran Mademoiselle (Jadranska magistrala | tel. 032 32 72 18 | restoran mademoiselle.business.site | €€)*. This restaurant has a romantic ambience with atmospheric lighting, candles, live music, tables by the waterside and good wine. Otherwise, you may stop at the *Marius (daily from noon | Jadranska magistrala | tel. 032 33 81 94 | €€)*, a restaurant on the shore with a terrace and great views. The food is delicious and you could literally jump from your seat onto the small beach and into the Adriatic. Some of the customers even wear swimsuits! *K4*

TIVAT

(J5) **Once a sleepy place, Tivat (9,400 residents) has been blessed with luxury and today is renowned for the superyachts berthed in its harbour.**

The town was controlled by the Venetians until 1797, followed by the Austro-Hungarian Empire that took advantage of Tivat's strategic location at the entrance to the bay to develop a naval base here. Warships were still anchored in Tivat in the 20th century: in Tito's era the town was the most important military base in the southern Adriatic. It was barred for tourism for a long time, and the town, with its nearby airport, only gradually opened up during the second half of the 20th century. EasyJet currently offers direct flights to the UK from Tivet.

SIGHTSEEING

YUGOSLAVIAN GENERAL CONSULATE

Yugoslavia has faded into history but the state still has a general consulate in Tivat. The telephone number is identical to the founding date of the Socialist Republic. There are all kinds of devotional objects such as flags, badges and old postcards on display. And, if you want to, you can be issued with a "genuine" Yugoslavian passport for a mere 10 euros. *Generalni konzulat SFRJ | daily 9am–5pm | Palih Borača 21c | FB: Generalni konzulat SFRJ | admission free | 1 hr*

Porto Montenegro is worth visiting, even if you don't own a yacht

PORTO MONTENEGRO ★

In 2006, the Canadian billionaire Peter Munk bought the run-down shipyards and promised to build Europe's best marina. No sooner said than done: Porto Montenegro is about to claim the top spot from Monte Carlo. Vast luxury yachts have their port home here. The Mediterranean Yacht Brokers Association displays the dream vessels every year in September at the *MYBA Pop-up Superyacht Show (yachtcharterfleet.com/events)*. Take a leisurely stroll along the marina to gawp at the display of luxury and wealth. It's not uncommon to see boats moored here that are up to 100m long, and their owners are often international celebrities. Next to the marina by the waterside the town has expanded with luxury apartments, costing 10,000 euros per square meter. Modern art is also on show: the promenade is adorned with several larger-than-life sculptures of a woman with huge feet in various poses. *porto montenegro.com*

MARITIME MUSEUM

Can you keep claustrophobia at bay when walking through a real submarine? This jewel of the Yugoslavian navy named *Heroj* (hero) is displayed in front of the former arsenal. The museum itself is little more than an old marine joinery with a pretty wooden ceiling and a few nice exhibits in the gallery, but the submarine alone is worth your visit. *Maritime Heritage Museum | Mon–Fri 9am–4pm, Sat 1–5pm | in Porto Montenegro | admission museum 3 euros, submarine an extra 2 euros | porto montenegro.com |* ⏱ *1 hr*

EATING & DRINKING

BIG BEN

If you love pizza – and who doesn't – you will appreciate this friendly restaurant. Their fish, meat, coffee and cakes are wonderful and the superb views from the terrace are thrown in for free. However, not everybody knows that this is also the ideal place for a late-evening glass of beer or to satisfy a night-time food craving (because they are open until 1am). *Šetalište Seljanovo 21 | tel. 067 37 14 66 | €€*

INSIDER TIP
Late pizza heaven

BUREGDZINICA "AS"

A lovely little snack bar with friendly service. The Turkish *borek* is delicious and they even serve freshly pressed juice at surprisingly reasonable prices. *Palih Boraca | €*

KONOBA BACCHUS

This restaurant is a little bit away from the others on the waterfront promenade. It is reasonably priced, open until late at night and popular with the locals. Good fish dishes: you should try the delicious squid stuffed with prawns. *Palih Borača | tel. 032 67 25 58 | FB: Konoba Bacchus | €€*

ONE – RESTAURANT & BAR

An attractive place to sip a prosecco and enjoy a meal by the waterside. They do excellent breakfasts as well. Located on the main promenade of Porto Montenegro. *Mobile 067 48 60 45 | FB: jettyone | €€–€€€)*

SHOPPING

In the labyrinthine streets of Porto Montenegro luxury boutiques such as Gaultier or Stella McCartney offer a glimpse of the world of the rich and beautiful. Here, you will learn the meaning of the Montenegrins' word for window shopping – *pariti oči* – or "watery eyes". On four dates during the summer the streets of Porto Montenegro host the farmers' market where you can wine and dine on organic produce; sample and buy honey, cheese, olive oil and ham from the mountain regions. *For dates visit portomontenegro.com.*

INSIDER TIP
Luxury farmers' market

BEACHES

In the nearby town of Oblatno, 16km away, *Almara Beach* provides sheer luxury. In addition to the standard sun loungers and sun canopies you can rent a "living room" – for 500 euros a day. This includes relaxation under a white canopy with sofas, chairs and plasma TV as well as a butler and cocktails.

If you haven't got that sort of cash, the public beaches in Tivat and nearby villages offer similar relaxation. Two sun loungers and a parasol often cost less than 10 euros here. South of Luka Kaliman harbour, almost on the edge of Tivat, is 🏊 *Belane Beach*. This is a pebble beach (as are most beaches here), but without any of the large or painful boulders that can often sour one's entry into the water. There is enough space, parasols are hired for an entire day, and changing rooms and showers are free. The beach is served by a proper café and – if you walk around with your smartphone – you may even get WiFi.

WELLNESS

There's a wide variety of luxury wellness centres in Porto Montenegro. At the *PMYC Pool (pmyc.portomontenegro.com)* non-residents pay 45 euros, but you can swim in a large pool with spectacular views and enjoy the club atmosphere, including music. They also offer sailing, rowing, SUP, yoga, golf, archery and more. The *Pura Vida* spa *(puravida-spa.com)* offers a 90-minute chocolate treatment for 120 euros. A full-body massage is priced from 35 euros.

FESTIVALS

OLIVE FESTIVAL

Young Montenegrins are rediscovering their cultural heritage: forgotten olive groves are being brought back to life and olives are harvested by hand and processed in ancient stone mills. The result: cold-pressed oil of the highest quality. In July, the female olive farmers of the *Boka* association *(maslinaboka.org)* celebrate their "Olive Day" in Tivat.

AROUND TIVAT

🔟 GOSPA OD ANĐELA
6km from Tivat, 10 mins by car on the coastal road

At the point where the coastal road from Tivat makes a sharp turn towards Kotor at the northern tip of the peninsula, the bay widens a little. Directly on the bend, in the village of Verige, you'll find on the shore the tiny and extremely photogenic Catholic church of *Gospa od Anđela*. ⛶ J4

🔢 LUŠTICA ★ ⚑
25km south of Tivat, 40 mins by car on the Adriatic coastal road and on local roads to Rose village

The Montenegrins call this 47km² peninsula southwest of Tivat the "Land of Olives". Olive trees have grown here since ancient times and most of the houses used to have their own mills; the people here lived with – and from – olives. Later Luštica came under the control of the military that guarded the entrance to the Bay of Kotor from here. Many residents departed and left behind abandoned villages. Now their grandchildren are returning to Luštica and with them are coming foreign investors. Luxury resorts, marinas and golf courses are springing up everywhere. The road along the north coast of the peninsula is particularly scenic, offering marvellous views of the Bay of Kotor. However, although most roads on Luštica are drivable, they can be narrow, windy and bumpy.

Gospa od Anđela is yet another church with sea views to die for

The interior of Luštica is also charming: deserted villages, stone houses in the shade of olive groves and clear, fresh air. In the middle of the peninsula *Obosnik Mountain* is 582m high, while on the northwestern side is the small spa town of *Rose*, Montenegro's "Saint-Tropez" where Serbian film stars have taken up residence. You, too, may feel like a celebrity when you stroll through this chic place! Roses and oleander grow on the stone walls of beautifully restored houses, palm trees give shade and the beach is just outside people's front door. Also, Herceg Novi, which you may be able to see from your bedroom window, is only a few minutes away by boat.

The 35km-long coastline is still fairly undeveloped and the unspoiled bays with their turquoise water lie secluded in the sun. Beautiful beaches include *Dobreč*, *Žanjice* and *Mirište*.

Arguably the best beach on Luštica is ⚓ *Plaža Arza* on the west coast's central section. However, getting there requires some effort: the tarmacked road ends at a car park 750m before the beach and, while you might be able to continue in the car, it is actually nicer to walk. Watch out for boulders when entering the water, otherwise this is an idyllic and usually quiet spot with few visitors. The water is crystal clear, so bring your snorkelling gear.

Modra Špilja, the Blue Cave, is on the south side of Luštica and can only be reached by sea. Boat tours leave from Tivat *(for information contact the tourist office on tel. 032 67 13 23 | tivat. travel)* and Herceg Novi *(Barkarioli | mobile 067 55 53 36)*. ▢ *H–J 5–6*

INSIDER TIP
The Blue Cave

THE ADRIATIC

MONTENEGRO'S RIVIERA

Beaches stretching for miles and picturesque bays, small sections of sandy coast hidden between the rocks and a green hinterland that almost reaches the shore – this is Montenegro's Adriatic coast.

The peaks of the Lovćen and Rumija soar behind delightful little harbour towns. A picturesque landscape stretches from Budva to the island of Ada Bojana: small fishing boats rocked gently by the waves, countless olive groves hidden in the beautiful hills, stone houses from another era and avenues lined with pine trees and cypresses.

Clear blue water and sunshine attract visitors to the fabulous beach at Petrovac na Moru

Past foreign conquerors left enchanting architectural traces in Budva, Stari Bar and the old town in Ulcinj – Illyrians, Romans, Venetians and Austrians occupied and defended these towns for centuries.

The Sozina Tunnel has shortened the travel time from the interior of the country to the coast by many miles. However, tourists from abroad will find the winding, 🐌 toll-free road from Virpazar more interesting. It runs through an especially picturesque area: on one side a lunar landscape, on the other breathtaking views of the sea.

THE ADRIATIC

MARCO POLO HIGHLIGHTS

★ **BUDVA OLD TOWN (STARI GRAD)**
Centuries-old Venetian heritage stands proudly on a small peninsula surrounded by old stone walls ➤ p. 66

★ **SV. STEFAN**
The most beautiful photo opportunity in the country and a meeting place for VIPs; what was once a fishermen's island has been transformed into a luxurious hotel ➤ p. 70

★ **PETROVAC NA MORU**
Magnificent houses on the promenade and palm trees on the beach: the small coastal village has retained much of its original charm ➤ p. 71

★ **BULJARICA**
Unimpaired views of the beach and sea from a place where the ground is too wet to support development ➤ p. 73

★ **STARI BAR**
A journey to the past: the ruins of Stari Bar lie at the foot of Mount Rumija ➤ p. 76

★ **VELIKA PLAŽA (GRAND BEACH)**
The longest beach in Montenegro is popular with children and surfers: the former love the shallow water; the latter enjoy the strong winds ➤ p. 79

Rvaši

Begova Glavica

Ljajkovići

Tuzi

TUZI

Hot

Prevlaka

Golubovci

Vuksanlekići

M2

Mataguži

M4

Vukpalaj-Bajzë

Bistrice

Jadranska magistrala

PODGORICA

Humsko blato

Vranjina

Jadranska magistrala

Ivanaj

Malo blato

SH1

Virpazar

Kamicë-Flakë

Seoca

Skadarsko jezero
Liqeni Shkodrës

Koplik

Limljani

Karanikići

BAR

Besa

Tuđemili

Gornja Briska

Sušanj

Martići

Bar
p.75

6 **Stari Bar** ★

Arbnež

7 Olive Trees

Veliki Mikulići

Zogaj

Shirokë

CRNA GORA / ЦРНА ГОРА

Međureč - Megjureç

8 Dobra Voda

SHQIPËRIA

8 Dubrava

Dabezići

Muriqan

SH41

8 Utjeha

Krute - Krytha

Vladimir - Katërkollë

Kruče

Ambula - Amulë

Dajç

M1

Velja Gorana

ULCINJ

Pentar

Bratica

Pistula - Pistulë

Darza - Darzë

SHQIPËRIA
VERIORE

Ulcinj (Ulqin)
p.76

Reç

Baks i Ri

🚲

4.5km, 15 mins

Velika Plaža ★

5 km
3.11 mi

Ada Bojana 9

Budva's old town is utterly charming

BUDVA

(⬜ L–M6) **No matter whether you drive down from Cetinje or arrive from Tivat, the first impression of the oldest city on the Montenegrin coast is spectacular.**

The historic heart of Budva (pop. 13,300) lies on a peninsula in the Adriatic that stretches towards the island of *Sv. Nikola*. The Venetians gave the old town its magnificent appearance in the 15th century; Budva was only slightly damaged in the 1979 earthquake and any traces of this have long disappeared.

No community in Montenegro has grown as quickly as Budva. The sell-out of property started immediately after the Balkan wars and today even the neighbouring mountains have been built on and integrated into the city. Living in the mountains with a pool and sea views is now all the rage because the city is often overcrowded – especially in summer. There is an acute lack of parking space, the roads around the town are jammed and water is short in high season. However, Budva remains a magnet for visitors, Serbs and Russians in particular: the town with the flashiest cars and highest prices on the coast attracts visitors with offers of long nights in the clubs, good food at the shoreline promenade and designer shops in the old town.

SIGHTSEEING

OLD TOWN (STARI GRAD) ★

Although the city's rulers changed frequently, architects from Venice made the strongest impact on the appearance of the pretty old town: they

MUZEJ GRADA BUDVE

The city museum, possibly the most beautiful in the country, has many exhibits from Budva's long history dating back to the fifth century BCE. Clay bowls and jugs, metal tools and coins from the Roman period are displayed in this house in the old town and give an excellent overview of what was once an Illyrian settlement. *Tue–Fri 9am–8pm, Sat/Sun 10am–5pm | Petrovića 11 | admission 3 euros | ⏱ 1 hr*

EATING & DRINKING

EKSPRESS FOOD

Self-service restaurants, so-called *ekspres restorani*, were popular under Tito because they allowed people to eat for less when on holiday. Today, almost all tourist towns still have a self-service restaurant with generous servings for a few euros. This one is managed in the style of a canteen, and is situated a few steps from *Slovenska Plaža Beach. Slovenska obala | €*

HOME OF GYROS BY NAKY'S

You get excellent Greek cuisine in this modern and bright restaurant with a friendly atmosphere. Servings are generous and the food is delicious and inexpensive. A few hundred metres from the town centre and therefore not overcrowded and with quick service. *29 Novembra | mobile 067 65 80 98 | €*

JADRAN – KOD KRSTA

This fish restaurant right at the harbour caters to all tastes: in addition

conquered Budva in 1442, built many churches as well as the well-preserved city wall, which they constructed on top of the remains of an ancient wall.

Every summer, the *Citadela (citadel | daily 9am–8pm | admission 3.50 euros | ⏱ 45 mins)* by the old town's main square, whose dramatic walls drop steeply down to the water, is turned into an 🏴 open-air stage for free concerts. In the old castle you can admire models of famous ships, such as Columbus's *Santa Maria*, but the highlight is definitely the incredible view across the Adriatic.

The ninth-century triple-nave Church of Saint John the Baptist *(Sv. Ivan)* and the bell tower *(Sahat kula)*, which was erected in 1867, are also worth seeing. Apart from its actual sights, the town is an attraction in itself with its countless old stone houses, small shops, cafés and restaurants.

to seafood, fresh fish and lobster, the menu lists typical Montenegrin meat dishes as well as reasonably priced set meals of the day.

INSIDER TIP
Eat well for less

Slovenska obala 10 | mobile 069 03 01 80 | restaurantjadran.com | €€–€€€

RESTORAN PORTO

Dine in a romantic location at the gates of the old town by the marina. Fish swim in a small tank and are freshly prepared, as is the scampi. *Marina Budva | tel. 033 45 15 98 | restoranporto.com | €€–€€€*

VERDE

A no-frills, quick-service, reasonably priced and overall good-quality restaurant. They also have vegetarian options and an English menu. *Velji Vinogradi | mobile 063 21 44 06 | €*

SPORT & ACTIVITIES

Budva's beaches like *Jaz* or *Slovenska plaža* are a paradise for fitness fanatics and sport fans. There is a wide range of activities on offer from bungee jumping and jet-skiing to surfing, snorkelling and diving. You can book "fish picnics" and boat excursions along the coast in many of the local travel agents.

BEACHES

JAZ

There is little risk of getting bored on this long pebble beach about 5km from Budva towards Tivat. You will find animation programmes for children, live music for adults, restaurants, bars, jet-ski, water ski and everything else. A ferry service connects you with Budva's old town. Only those who seek peace and quiet should stay away! However, everybody loves the crystal-clear water. A third of the beach is declared nudist.

MOGREN I & II

The two beaches, separated from each other by a steep rock face, are only a few minutes away from the Hotel Avala and are much more peaceful than Jaz town beach and Slovenska plaža. A handful of cafés and pubs serve refreshments and it is also possible to hire pedal boats here.

SLOVENSKA PLAŽA

The long shingle beach stretches for a few hundred feet from the harbour to the end of the bay at Budva in the direction of Bečići. It offers a wide range of restaurants as well as many sporting opportunities.

FESTIVALS

Every year at the end of August, Buljarica Beach at Budva becomes a big stage for the four-day *Sea Dance Festival (day ticket from 20 euros | seadancefestival.me)* with rock, pop, electro and dance.

NIGHTLIFE

Budva is one large nightclub. The Montenegrins love loud music, and it booms out of every beach bar until late at night. Most of the clubs can be found along *Slovenska obala*.

AROUND BUDVA

1 BEČIĆI

4km/5 mins from Budva on the E80

To this day the residents of this coastal village (pop. 2,000) are proud that their 2km of 🏖️ beach was voted the most beautiful in the Mediterranean in Paris, 1936. The great advantage is that this pebble beach is kept immaculately clean, especially in the cordoned-off section where you have to pay for sun loungers. There is easy access to the water and the promenade is great for strolling.

Foreign investors have built luxurious four- and five-star hotels overlooking the beach. Spas and relaxation, caviar and lobster are all on the agenda there. The *Spa Resort Bečići (Ive Lole Ribara | tel. 033 47 14 50 | sparesortbecici.com)* offers wellness and bungee jumping – also to non-residents. 🗺️ M6

2 PRŽNO

7km/10 mins from Budva on the E80

It is also possible to spend wonderful sunny days in the appealing Bay of Pržno on the coastal road towards Petrovac and Ulcinj. A couple of *konobas* (small typical restaurants) at the eastern end of the beach invite visitors

Enjoy balmy summer evenings in Budva with a sundowner by the old town walls

to stay for a while. *Konoba More* with its stone walls, a water-side terrace and exquisite fish dishes is highly recommended *(Obala 18 | tel. 033 46 82 55 | konobamore.me | €€)*. The *Maestral (tel. 033 41 01 00 | maestral.me)* has one of the many hotel casinos that are especially popular with weekend tourists from Italy. ⌂ M6

🔳 SV. STEFAN ★

9km/15 mins from Budva on the E80 and E65

Even if you don't want to stay or eat in the resort of Sv. Stefan and Miločer, you absolutely have to visit it for a leisurely stroll! Originally, the island measuring 1.6 hectares was not connected to the mainland about 100m away. The promontory, developed in the 19th century, was supposed to make life easier for the fishermen on the island. However, the local fishermen were removed in 1956 and work started to convert on Sv. Stefan to a hotel island. From an outsider's viewpoint, the compact 15th-century village remained unchanged. But life inside in the almost 100 stone houses was transformed into pure luxury. In 1960, the former Yugoslavia's most expensive hotel opened and it has since attracted the likes of Claudia Schiffer, Silvester Stallone and Sophia Loren.

In 2009, the architectural gem was sold. Investors came and went, and the hotel remained closed for a long

Thankfully, Petrovac has no ugly hotel blocks right behind the beach

while. The enchanted island with its red-roofed stone houses merely remained the most photographed symbol of Montenegro. The outlook from the *viewing platform* on the main street of the "Pearl of the Adriatic" has been photographed millions of times.

After it was sold to a new owner and luxuriously renovated, the resort re-opened in 2013 as Hotel *Aman Sv. Stefan*. The Serbian tennis star Novak Đoković got married in 2014 in the small island church, and the photos were sent around the world.

Miločer, the former summer residence of the Yugoslavian kings, which was built in the 1930s, is also part of the hotel complex. The main residence is directly on a small bay, and from its restaurant terrace you can enjoy the view of Sv. Stefan. Other small houses are in a large park. The fragrance of cypress, oleander and pines accompany you on the way to your room.

Several restaurants are situated between Sv. Stefan and Miločer. Directly opposite the island, the *Olive (mobile 069 1879 88 | olivetaste.com | €€–€€€)* serves Mediterranean cuisine. Its terrace in the evening is particularly atmospheric and romantic and the view of Sv. Stefan is unique! But don't worry, eating here is quite affordable. In Miločer Park, the renowned Japanese restaurant *Nobu (mobile 069 13 31 58 | noburestaurants.com | €€€)* serves Japanese fusion cuisine. *▥ M6*

SIDER TIP
Utterly romantic

PETROVAC NA MORU

(▥ N6) **The tranquil little town of ★ Petrovac na Moru lies in a small bay directly beneath the coastal road that leads from Sv. Stefan to Sutomore and Bar.**

The settlement originally consisted of a series of Venetian houses right on the bay – *na moru* means "on the sea". The promenade is still beautiful thanks to these houses that have stood here for centuries. The forefathers of the inhabitants of Petrovac (pop. 1,400), who are members of the powerful Paštrovići clan, came down from the mountains above today's coastal road and some of their stone houses have been preserved to this day.

Although there are many villas, apartments and small hotels in Petrovac, its location between the road and sea has to a large extent prevented the town from falling victim to the country's construction craze. Steps lead down to the water from the Medinski krš district shortening the distance to the *town beach*. However, it is much more pleasant to wander through the small alleyways and breathe in the perfume of the Mediterranean plants. There are palm trees and cypresses at the beach, and cafés, pubs and restaurants wait to welcome their guests not even 30m away. You can settle down on one of the *old benches under the trees next to the beach – a pleasant alternative to the nearby sun loungers that cost 10 euros a day. And you will still have the same view of the sea.

The two small monasteries in the town (14th and 15th century) are beautifully illuminated at night. There is a church on the island of *Sv. Neđelja* just off the coast; it is said that a sailor built it out of gratitude for having been rescued from the sea. There are daily boat excursions to the island.

As is the case with many other towns on the coast, Petrovac is overcrowded during high season. It is much more beautiful here – and much less expensive – in May and June when the broom is in full bloom, or in September when the water is almost lukewarm.

SIGHTSEEING

KASTEL LASTVA

The location of the small fort in the sea in the west of the bay is quite unique: a great destination for a walk and the ultimate photo opportunity. *Admission free*

EATING & DRINKING

FORTUNA

What makes this restaurant so special is not only the excellent food but also the "roof" of leaves of the rubber plants that flourish in the garden. There are also sea views. The first-rate fillet steak and pasta as well as seafood and fish & chips are highly recommended. *Obala | mobile 069 65 50 00 | FB: Fortunapetrovac | €€*

LAZARET

This restaurant next to the fortress on the promenade serves delicious pizza, lasagne and other dishes with only a short wait. Its location provides fabulous views, and night owls can enjoy themselves here until 2am. *Obala | mobile 069 02 61 57 | €*

PLAŽNI BAR MEDIN

A terrace, wooden tables, benches and chairs, drinks, a good beer, generous servings of grilled meats and reasonable prices – and all of that almost on the beach. This friendly establishment, whose name translates as "beach bar", is really a full-blown restaurant. *Lučice | mobile 069 45 63 80 | FB: medinbarpetrovac | €*

VILA CASTIO

Dana Đuković-Kučko learned all there is to know about cooking and serving while working in a top hotel abroad. She returned to Petrovac after almost 30 years, opened her gourmet restaurant with only six tables on the promenade and named it after the old name of the town. Dana specialises in all kinds of fish and seafood. *Nika Anđusa 16 | tel. 067 45 67 00 | €€*

BEACHES

LUČICE

This shingle beach (about 250m long and 30m wide) is surrounded by two high green slopes and is just past the Hotel Rivijera on the way out of Petrovac. A water slide is a special attraction for children. It's at its quietest on weekdays or during low season.

Perched on a rock, Kastel Lastva guards Petrovac na Moru and its bay

AROUND PETROVAC NA MORU

4 BULJARICA ⭐

3km/5 mins from Petrovac on the E80

This long stretch of bay south of Petrovac is free of hotels – a rarity in Montenegro. The subterranean springs have prevented the development of Buljarica, as it would be too expensive to drain the ground. So the 2km-long beach gleams in the sunshine in all its pristine glory.

The eponymous village is located below the coastal road and is surrounded by lush greenery. Tourists who stay here have a ten-minute walk to the beach and can enjoy friendly staff and low prices at local restaurants.

Health is the top priority at the *Savojo Hotel (mobile 067 22 14 42 | savojo.me)* right on the coast: the owner is a practitioner of sports medicine and his son is a chiropractor; they offer physiotherapy programmes as well as yoga and other forms of therapy by the beach, also for non-residents. They also serve organic products and wine from their own cellar. 📖 *N6*

INSIDER TIP
Ommmm!

Stari Bar transports you 1,000 years into the past

5 SUTOMORE

13km/20 mins from Petrovac on the E80

The name of this small town (pop. 2,000) can be traced back to the Italian *sotto mare*, meaning "the lower sea". The mile-long sandy beach remained unspoiled by tourism until two hotels opened their doors here in the 1960s; most of the guests at the time were package-holiday tourists who were not very demanding. The wind and water were sufficient to make them forget the shortcomings of the Socialist-era concrete buildings.

Today Sutomore has countless reasonably priced accommodation options; there are small hotels and apartment houses all the way up to the coast road. However, you will only find peace and quiet higher up the mountain – as so often happens in Montenegro, the beach turns into one long disco at night and every pub plays its own kind of music at full volume.

The medieval *church dedicated to Saint Tekla* is an interesting cultural monument in Sutomore. An Orthodox and Catholic altar stand side by side as a sign of religious tolerance.

The town is crowded in the summer months – especially at weekends when all of Podgorica migrates to the Adriatic coast. 🕮 *07*

BAR

(□ P7) **The town has developed rapidly in recent decades and is no longer a historic gem. Bar (pop. 18,000) now has a network of wide streets and boulevards. There are high-rise buildings and shopping malls shooting up all over.**

Bar's population is young – university courses at the faculties of journalism and business administration are sought after by students from all parts of Montenegro. The city is also increasingly becoming the cultural and economic centre of the southern Adriatic. The marina has moorings for 900 vessels and the harbour is abuzz with activity. The permanent ferry connections to Bari, as well as the railway line from Belgrade, bring many tourists into the city. Although most are headed to one of the nearby vacation spots, Bar still profits from them.

SIGHTSEEING

KING NIKOLA'S PALACE
Artefacts from many centuries are on display in the former summer residence of King Nikola on the waterfront promenade. On the top floor, you can admire the king's former living quarters. *Mon–Sat 9am–8pm | Šetalište Kralja Nikole | admission 1 euro | ⊘ 1½ hrs*

EATING & DRINKING

You will find a slew of restaurants in various price categories on the promenade, where you can enjoy your meal with views of the sailing boats.

KNJAŽEVA BAŠTA
You can dine in the luxurious surroundings of the gardens of the former royal residence. Mussels and wine are particularly recommended. *Jovana Tomasevica | tel. 030 31 26 01 | knjazevabasta.com | €€-€€€*

RESTORAN MORNAR
Here you get delicious food across the board – from fish and seafood to meat and vegetarian options – at fair prices. Servings are generous and the service is quick. Perfect for a lunch break because this place is not yet as overrun in summer as many other locations in the region. *Jovana Tomasevica | mobile 067 18 14 44 | restoranmornar.me | €€*

SHOPPING

The large supermarkets in the centre of Bar offer excellent possibilities for shopping. On no account should you miss the *farmers' market (daily 7am–2pm | Bar pijaca)*, which is also held in the city centre. The fresh fish attracts local people from across the region. Vast quantities of fruit and vegetables, heavy hams, honey and olive oil, bay leaves and rosemary – the market offers a colourful selection of all the region's produce and the aroma is heavenly! You simply must get some delicious goat's or sheep's milk cheese, of which there are many varieties. *INSIDER TIP Ewe's cheese*

AROUND BAR

6 STARI BAR ★
4km/5 mins from Bar

New life has been breathed into this town that was long deserted, even if it retains the feel of a ghost town in low season. Old *(stari)*, historic Bar is located north of Bar at the beginning of the ascent to Mount Rumija. The origins of the city, which is surrounded by a mighty wall, can be traced back to the 11th century, when Bar was part of the Serbian coastal state of Zeta. The *city gate*, whose façade was reconstructed in the 14th century, dates from this period. *St George's Cathedral* was erected in the Romanesque Gothic style in the 12th century. The remains of an even older church have been discovered beneath its walls.

There are also traces of the time the Turks occupied the city, such as the old *hammam (June–Oct accessible round the clock | admission 1 euro)*. In the main street is the cosy *Karađuzović* confectionery, where you don't just get a good mocha but also the best baklava in the region *(Staro Barska Čarsija)*.

INSIDER TIP
Indulge yourself

Stari Bar is also home to the olive farmers' association *(oliveoilmonte negro.me)*. In November, after the harvest, they hold their *Maslinijada* olive festival here. *P7*

7 OLIVE TREES
5km/5 mins from Bar

Between Bar and Ulcinj there are about 175,000 olive trees, many of them have been here for 2,000 years. The oldest tree – also one of the oldest trees in the world – is reputed to be 2,200 years old. It is near the village of Tomba on the old road from Stari Bar to Ulcinj. *P7*

8 DOBRA VODA, DUBRAVA & UTJEHA
15km/20mins from Bar to Utjeha

The drive to the bays is worthwhile: the sea and lovely beaches are close by, you are surrounded by pine trees and cypresses and apartments and hotels are comparatively cheap. The chirping of the crickets is an extra bonus! It is most beautiful here at the end of May when the blossoming broom turns the entire region into a sea of yellow. Dobra Voda is not directly by the waterside, but mainly situated above the through road. It offers stunning views of the Adriatic, for example from the terrace of the *Kalamper* restaurant *(Dobra Voda | tel. 030 34 18 33 | €–€€)*, which serves seafood and grilled meats. They even have a plunge pool for children up to the age of ten. *P–Q7*

INSIDER TIP
Broom blossom in May

ULCINJ (ULQIN)

(R8) **Nowhere else on the eastern Adriatic are the beaches as long and sandy as they are around Ulcinj**

(pop. 10,000), the southernmost town on the Montenegrin coast. In the town itself it almost feels as if you are in Albania.

From time immemorial, the sea has washed sand ashore that is rich in salts; created by the erosion of quartz boulders, it reaches the coast with the flow of the Montenegrin Albanian border river, the Bojana.

In addition to its beaches, Ulcinj draws tourists with its Middle Eastern character. You will notice this immediately by the busy atmosphere and people's traditional dress, by the bazar, the style of the buildings and the call of the muezzin. Starting in the Middle Ages, migrants from the Slavic principality of Zeta settled here along with Albanians coming from the south; they now make up more than three-quarters of the population.

SIGHTSEEING

STARI GRAD (OLD TOWN)

Despite the steep ascent, it is worth the effort: the foundations of the old town, standing proudly above the newer part of Ulcinj, and the massive walls of the *citadel* have their roots in Illyrian and Greek eras and were later altered time and time again by Byzantine, Turkish and Venetian inhabitants and conquerors. The *Balšić Tower (Balšića kula)*, on the other hand, was built in the days of the medieval state of Raška. And the views of the coast are spectacular!

GRADSKI MUZEJ (CITY MUSEUM)

Little Turkey in Montenegro: the museum, housed in the old Turkish

Narrow alleyways in the elevated old town of Ulcinj

prison, exhibits many objects that recount the history of the city, including old Muslim gravestones and Turkish cannonballs. Descriptions are provided in English. *Daily 8am–8pm | at the western gate to the old town | admission 2.50 euros | ⊙ 1 hr*

EATING & DRINKING

In Ulcinj, many Albanians have become successful restaurateurs and it is possible to choose between traditional Balkan cuisine (*ćevapčići* and *ražnjići*) and an excellent variety of fish dishes. No matter whether you select the *Antigona (old town | mobile 069 15 41 17 | FB: Restaurant Antigona | €€)* by the waterside with its wonderful views, the *Teuta (old town | mobile 069 29 33 47 | restaurant-teuta.com | €€)* with its 130m² ter-race or the *Aragosta II (Steva Đakonovića Čiče | mobile 069 83 33 46 | €€)*, which is open round the clock and serves freshly caught fish under pine trees on the beach, you will be delighted by their excellent value for money. You can also eat well and inexpensively in the numerous bars and pizzerias at the Grand Beach, *Velika plaža*.

INSIDER TIP
Delicacies round the clock

SHOPPING

LOVAC ORGANIC EXTRA VIRGIN OLIVE OIL

In the *Lovac* restaurant on the Grand Beach you can fill a few bottles of premium olive oil to take away at a good price. If you are shopping for larger quantities, bargaining may be an option. *Velika plaža*

SPORT & ACTIVITIES

Ulcinj is an ideal location for surfers and kitesurfers because of the strong winds. You'll find most facilities at the Grand Beach. In the Bojana Delta the fishermen still cast their nets in the traditional way and you can be there to witness it.

BEACHES

CITY BEACHES

Gradska plaža, the city beach, is also known as *Mala plaža* (Little Beach) and is usually very crowded. There are several small beaches with deep water near the cliffs to the left of the sandy beach. A small nudist beach lies tucked away in the shade of some cypresses and there is also a very popular *Ladies' Beach (Ženska plaža)* where the sulphur, radium and sea salts are said to have healing properties.

AGAINST THE CURRENT

When the snowmelt in the Albanian mountains makes the Drim (the Bojana River's main tributary) swell at the end of winter, the main river is no longer able to flow in its customary direction. Instead of flowing from Lake Skadar into the Adriatic, the river on the border of Montenegro and Albania starts to flow upstream. The fishermen who spread their trapeze nets in the Bojana Delta are guaranteed a fine catch, which is swiftly sold to tourists on the Grand Beach!

Traditional fishing methods are still used in the Bojana Delta

VELIKA PLAŽA (GRAND BEACH)

The Grand Beach or *Velika plaža* is 12km long, but why are Montenegrins so proud of this small stretch of land? In a country that is dominated by stony or at best pebble beaches, the fine dark sand is like gold dust, and especially as there is so much of it in one place. It is divided into sections that have been named after their owners, and in most cases these sections have their own campsite, bar and restaurant, e.g. *Miami, Copacabana or Safari Beach*.

AROUND ULCINJ (ULQIN)

🖪 ADA BOJANA

16km/20 mins from Ulcinj on the R17
This island in the delta of the Albanian–Montenegrin border river east of Ulcinj can only be reached from the mainland via a bridge. The longest nudist beach in Montenegro is here, and there are campsites too. In spite of the middling accommodation, the island has developed into a paradise for tourists who are nature and sports enthusiasts. The wind, water and sun also create ideal conditions for kitesurfers, including beginners who can go on courses at the kitesurfing school (*kiteloop.net*). 〰 S8

INSIDER TIP
Brave the winds

CETINJE, LAKE SKADAR & PODGORICA

TWO CAPITAL CITIES & A HUGE LAKE

Montenegro's former capital Cetinje has remained its spiritual centre: the head of the country's Orthodox Church resides here, and the mausoleum of the venerated poet Prince Njegoš in the Lovćen Mountains is only a short distance away.

Cetinje is the gateway to the interior of the country and to the north (towards Nikšić, Danilovgrad or the Bosnian border). The more-than-a-century-old network of roads shows how important the city once was – and still is – for the residents of the region.

Between Cetinje and Podgorica you get great views of the River Rijeka Crnojevića

Today, lively Podgorica is Montenegro's capital and its political, business and cultural centre. The drive on the old road from Cetinje to Podgorica is an unforgettable highlight of any trip to Montenegro because Lake Skadar, on the plain below, glitters in the sunlight in hues of green and dark blue. Hundreds of bird species nest around the largest lake on the Balkan Peninsula. Only a few decades ago, the people living around it were almost completely cut off from the cities on the coast, but now they have a good business offering boat tours.

CETINJE, LAKE SKADAR & PODGORICA

Banjamovića
Tomići
Orasi
Vuči Do
Vojkovići
R17
Releze
1 Njeguši ★
CRNA GORA / ЦРНА ГОРА
Žanjev Do
Dubovik
Kosijeri
Cetinje ★ p.84
2 ⟵25km, 50 mins
Dobrska Župa
Njegoš Mausoleum ★
R25
Donji Ulići
CETINJE
Bjeloši
M10
Rijeka Crnojevića
Obod 4 3
Šišići
Majstori
Riječani
Gorovići
Boguti
Lapčići
Obzovica
Lastva Grbaljska
Brajići
Građani
M1
Budva
Pržno
Sveti Stefan
Ovtočići
Gornji Brčeli
BUDVA
M2

MARCO POLO HIGHLIGHTS

★ **CETINJE**
The former capital with its historic embassies is one big open-air museum ➤ p.84

★ **NJEGUŠI**
The dry-cured ham from this village is famous around the world ➤ p.87

★ **NJEGOŠ MAUSOLEUM**
The views from the country's landmark stretch far across the Adriatic towards Italy ➤ p.87

★ **LAKE SKADAR (SKADARSKO JEZERO)**
Countless bird species and huge shoals of fish – the perfect incentive for a boat tour ➤ p.88

These walls protect a treasured manuscript and a famous billiard table: Biljarda

CETINJE

(□ L–M4) **The historical capital city ★ Cetinje (pop. 14,000) feels like a large open-air museum.**

The city is full of traces of the years following the first independence of Montenegro after the 1878 Congress of Berlin: embassies of all of the major powers of the time, who maintained contacts with King Nikola I, are scattered throughout the town. The king craftily arranged for his daughters to marry into the courts of many of the continent's royal families and, in this way, made the small country more influential than it would ever be again.

The history of the community, built on a barren field of karst, dates back to the 15th century when the first Montenegrin ruler, Ivan Crnojević, established his residence here while retreating from the Turks. The spiritual and political leader had the monastery in Cetinje built in 1484. At the end of the 19th century the sleepy metropolis was given the new appearance that it has retained to this day: low houses and straight streets lined with lime trees and acacias. It is hard to believe that this small town was once the country's focal point!

SIGHTSEEING

Cetinje's main sight is not one particular building, instead it is the atmosphere of the small town that is so full of history. It's worth taking a tour of the town. The embassies of what were then the most powerful European states – France *(Njegoševa)*, Russia *(Vuka Mićunovića)*, England *(Trg Novice Cerovića)* and the Austro-Hungarian Empire *(Pivljanina)* – are particularly impressive. Almost opposite the French embassy is the radiant *Blue Palace (Plavi Dvorac | Njegoševa)*: Prince Danilo's former residence in a dazzling blue is in a magnificent location in the city park. The building, which was constructed at the end of the 19th century, later served as the model for the other palaces of the Montenegrin royal family. Today, the Ministry of Culture resides in the Blue Palace.

Around the corner is the unimposing *Vlach Church (Vlaška crkva | Baja Pivljanina)* from 1450, the town's oldest building. In the Middle Ages, shepherds let their flocks graze here. According to legend, the mortal remains of the 17th-century military commander Bajo Pivljanin and his wife are buried beneath the church.

Follow the Baja Pivljanina in a southeasterly direction. The white *Royal Theatre (Zetski Dom | V Proleterske Brigade)* with its colonnaded portal has been used for a variety of purposes from museum to library and theatre, but today you can only admire the exterior. Erected on nearby Dvorski Trg Square on the ruins of the historical monastery that was destroyed in 1886, the small but pretty *Palace Chapel (Crkva na Ćipuru)* now houses the coffins with the mortal remains of King Nikola 🐷 and Queen Milena.

At the city's central museum administration in the Government House *(Vladin dom)* tourists can buy 🐷 discounted combined tickets *(10 euros)*

for the Montenegrin Art Gallery, the Njegoš Museum, King Nikola Museum and the History Museum, The opening times of all the museums are (unless stated otherwise below): *April–Oct Mon–Sat 9am–5pm, Nov–March 9am–4pm | mnmuseum.org*

MUZEJ KRALJA NIKOLE (KING NIKOLA MUSEUM)

The former palace has been a museum since 1926: the ruler's parade, hunting and trophy weapons are all displayed on the ground floor. A tour of the first floor, with the living quarters and work rooms decorated with the original furniture and paintings, gives an impression of the everyday life of King Nikola. *Trg Novice Cerovića | admission 5 euros | 🕐 1 hr*

BILJARDA (NJEGOŠ MUSEUM)

The former residence of the poet Prince Bishop Petar Njegoš includes books from his library and his own writings – including the manuscript of the *The Mountain Wreath* – as well as the billiard table that was to give the building its name. It was transported on the back of a donkey up the stony road from Kotor at the beginning of the 19th century. *Trg Novice Cerovića | admission 3 euros | 🕐 1 hr*

UMJETNIČKI MUZEJ CRNE GORE (ART MUSEUM)

The exhibition shows works by classical and modern Yugoslavian and Montenegrin artists. The collection dates back to the 17th century. The highlight of the exhibition is the *Icon of Mary the Mother of God by*

You really must try the famous dry-cured ham from Njeguši

The art gallery was named after Dado Đurić, the most famous Montenegrin painter. In addition to local artists, works by foreign artists are exhibited and the programme also includes concerts and talks. *April–Oct Tue–Sun 10am–2pm, 5–9pm, Nov–March Tue–Sat 10am–5pm | Njegoševa | admission 4 euros | ⏱ 2 hrs*

INSIDER TIP
Live art

Philernmos, the patron saint of the Order of Knights of St John. The golden portrait is one of the most important sacred relics of Christianity. It is said to have been painted by Luke the Evangelist. *Novice Cerovića | admission 4 euros | ⏱ 1–2 hrs*

CRNOGORSKA GALERIJA UMJETNOSTI MIODRAG DADO ĐURIĆ (ART GALLERY)

The former Trgopromet department store, a linear building and showpiece of Socialist-era architecture, now accommodates the country's modern art in all its genres: sculpture and fine arts, happenings, performances as well as digital and multimedia works.

EATING & DRINKING

BELVEDER ⚑

This restaurant boasts panoramic views from the terrace that sweep across Lake Skadar as far as Albania. It first opened its doors as a coffee house in 1888, but now you should try the tasty lamb cooked under the *sač*. *Magistralni put E 80 bb | when entering Cetinje from the direction of Podgorica | tel. 067 56 92 17 | €€*

RESTAURANT KOLE

Here you will quickly recover from the onslaught of history and culture which you will have enjoyed in the old capital. Quick and friendly service, delicious food, fair prices, an entertaining design and mainly frequented by local people; what more do you want? The predominantly meat-based dishes are tasty. *Bulevar Crnogorskih Junaka 12 | mobile 069 60 66 60 | restaurantkole.me | €–€€*

SPORT & ACTIVITIES

AVANTURISTIČKI PARK 👥

A visit to this adventure park in the Lovćen Mountains is a thrilling outdoor experience for kids and their parents. Amidst unspoiled nature you can climb, slide, crawl and jump over obstacles. Following a thorough briefing (in English) you can conquer climbing gardens, hiking trails and zip-lines with varying degrees of difficulty so that even small children can have fun while being safe. You can spend hours here, which is why there is also a restaurant on site. *Daily 9am–6pm | Ivanova korita bb National Park Lovćen | 14km outside town | FB: Avanturistički park*

AROUND CETINJE

1 NJEGUŠI ★

20km/30 mins from Cetinje on the P1 (mountain road)

The birthplace (pop. 200) of the poet and prince, Petar Njegoš, is 20km from Cetinje towards the Bay of Kotor. A special smoking technique has made the ham produced by the farmers in the village famous far beyond the boundaries of Montenegro. You can also buy smoked cheese, wine and home-distilled spirits here – look for the signs *(pršut, sir, vino, rakija)*. The house Njegoš was born in is only open in summer and can be found on the main road – there is a signpost. *Kod Pera Na Bukovicu (tel. 041 76 00 55 | €–€€)*, the oldest pub in the region, serves all the local specialities – and also guarantees a spectacular view of the Lovćen. *L4*

2 NJEGOŠ MAUSOLEUM ★ ▶

25km/50 mins from Cetinje on a mountain road

Montenegro's poet prince, Njegoš, lies buried in an oversized mausoleum on the second highest summit in the Lovćen range, the Jezerski vrh (1,660m). The *Njegoš Mausoleum* is flanked by two giant black marble statues of women and an equally imposing statue of Njegoš himself. A mosaic made from 20,000 gilt pieces decorates the ceiling inside.

From the Njegoš Mausoleum a signposted hiking trail leads to the summit. The ascent lasts around four hours and the return hike approximately three and a half. From Cetinje you drive to the summit on a narrow, tarmacked road. When you arrive, you still have to climb 461 steps before you can enjoy the magnificent view over Montenegro. Breathe in deeply and look out over the Bay of Kotor, Lake Skadar and all the way to Albania! *May–Sept daily 8am–6pm | admission 3 euros, plus another 3 euros for the national park | ⏱ 1 hr incl. ascent and descent via steps | L5*

3 RIJEKA CRNOJEVIĆA

17km/30 mins from Cetinje

Those who take the old road from Cetinje to Podgorica will be rewarded with spectacular views of Lake Skadar. The beautiful green river – which is also named *Rijeka Crnojevića* – winds its way into the lake. At first sight, the hamlet with its ruined buildings looks a bit odd, but the centre with the incredibly

INSIDER TIP
Over the bridge

steep stone bridge is charming. You can eat well in the friendly *Nowy Most* restaurant *(mobile 069 76 22 28 | €€)*, which serves tasty fish platters. *N4*.

4 OBOD

18km/30 mins from Cetinje on the M 2.3

The hamlet of Obod (pop. 200) lies on a small hill opposite Rijeka Crnojevića. Although there is still an Orthodox church and a few old stone houses, you will hardly see any people. For Montenegrins, this seemingly inconspicuous place is of great historic significance. In 1475, Prince Ivan Crnojević and his entourage escaped from the Turks by retreating from Lake Skadar to Obod. Only a few years after Johannes Gutenberg had invented book printing, his son Đurađ established the first printing press in southeast Europe here in the year 1493; it was later transferred to Cetinje. The first book to be printed in Cyrillic script was produced in Obod. *N4*

LAKE SKADAR (SKADARSKO JEZERO)

(N–S 3–6) **Gardens covered in vines, dilapidated churches in the valley and white-walled cemeteries set in lush meadows and fertile fields: the residents of ★ Lake Skadar live in harmony with nature and reap the benefits of its bounty.**

For centuries, rebellious Montenegrin clans and Turkish conquerors fought over this body of water. Today, the border between Montenegro and Albania runs down the middle of the lake, which is named after Skadar (Shkoder in Albanian), the most important city on its shores. The lake is fed by subterranean springs and has the same temperature throughout the year even though the ice-cold water of the *Morača* flows into it on the west side. It is the largest lake on the Balkan Peninsula. After the snow thaw in spring, it expands to cover an area of

BIRD LAND

Montenegro's diverse countryside attracts a variety of bird species that is unrivalled in Europe. On Lake Skadar alone there are almost 300 different species, and a quarter of a million birds from northern Europe overwinter in this region. You'll even find pelicans on the lake, which is also home to Europe's second biggest cormorant colony. Birdwatching tours are organised here and in Biogradska gora National Park, in Durmitor, where ornithologists have discovered more than 100 species, or in the marshlands around Ulcinj. For more information, please visit *lakeskadar.me*.

Do you think the fishermen know how deep Lake Skadar is?

more than 500km² and is still over 300km² in autumn. The Montenegrin part of the lake was declared a national park in 1983 while the Albanian section has been protected since 2005.

The surface of the lake is covered with water lilies and other rare plants and glistens in many colours. Ibises and storks gather at the edge in the shallow water, and there is a wonderful fragrance from the laurel trees on the lake shore and the towering chestnut trees. The *Rijeka Crnojevića* winds its way fjord-like to the lake. Old fishing villages and convents where nuns dressed in black carry out their work in silence are the kinds of scenes from a world that is no more than two hours away from the hustle and bustle of the tourist towns on the coast. The best way to explore this beautiful lake is on

a boat trip to *Grmožur* islet which has the ruins of an Ottoman fort. There are countless operators, but one of the best is *Boat Milica (from 25 euros/hr | mobile 067 21 16 98 | boatmilica.com).*

INSIDER TIP Natural photo opportunities

WHERE TO GO ON LAKE SKADAR

⑤ VIRPAZAR

It will become immediately apparent why the largest settlement (pop. 1,000) on the Montenegrin shore of Lake Skadar held a strategically important position for centuries. It was once an island – and was the last bastion against the Ottomans. If you follow the dead-straight railway embankment that was built in the 1970s for a mile or so towards Podgorica, you will

Once strategically important, Virpazar is now an attractive lakeside village

see the 🐗 *Lesendra fortress (admission free)* on the left-hand side. The Turkish stronghold was built to secure the conquests of the pashas in Istanbul. Today, two bridges connect the fishing village with the coast.

From the end of April, when the irises and water lilies are in full bloom, the season for private tours begins among the reeds by the lake shore. You will know that you are in the right place when, after entering the village, a group of local people comes your way, offering you the "very best" and "cheapest" boat trips in a friendly but persistent manner. It is best to take your time to compare prices before making the choice you are really happy with.

The weekly market that gave the village its name (Virpazar means "lively market") is held on Friday and is full of colour. In a chatter of Montenegrin and Albanian, peasant women and fishermen offer delicacies of the area from fresh oil and carp to tomatoes and peppers. You can even collect some natural products yourself near Virpazar. If you drive in the direction of Rijeka Crnojevića and leave the main road for a short while, you will find 🐗 plenty of wild herbs such as sage, rosemary and thyme. ⊞ *O5*

INSIDER TIP
Become a herbalist

6 MURIĆI

Do you have a head for heights? From Virpazar a winding road leads through the mountains into the village of Murići. The area that you are travelling through looks like a moonscape and Skadar Lake glimmers to the left of the route. Similar to other villages in this region, Murići has Catholic churches and mosques right next to each other – many of the Albanian residents here are Catholics. The village is slightly higher up in the mountains while accommodation and restaurants are directly by the lake. The Virpazar–Murići route also serves as a cycle trail (you can get more information in the visitor centre in Virpazar). After Murići the road continues over Mount Rumija (1,584m) to Ulcinj and Ada Bojana. *P6*

7 BEŠKA

Swallows, snakes and stones – that was what constituted the tiny island in the southern part of Lake Skadar until 2004. Then Orthodox nuns arrived and settled in the convent that had been deserted for 300 years. They have had electricity for a few years now but there is still no running water. The barren island smells of rosemary and sage, the sun beats down and the nuns work and pray until late at night. And they welcome day-trippers who bring some change to their monotonous life. Two- and eight-hour boat trips are offered locally. Most of the excursion boats depart from Virpazar or Murići in the morning. Information is available from the visitor centre in Virpazar. *P–Q6*

8 ŽABLJAK

It is possible that the myth of Montenegro's Black Mountain has its origins in this sleepy little village (whose name mustn't be confused with that of the famous town in the mountains of northern Montenegro) 23km from Virpazar. Before the Ottomans started making life difficult for the founder of the state, Ivan Crnojević and his companions had their ancestral seat in this fortress on the edge of Lake Skadar. However, after the Ottoman troops had conquered Podgorica and Skadar, the members of the Crnojević clan were forced to give up their vulnerable retreat on the plain and move to highlands of Obod and Cetinje at the end of the 15th century. A trail leads up to the well-preserved *fortress ruins (admission free)* in 15 minutes. From the top there is a magnificent view of the surrounding landscape – especially after the snow thaw in spring when the flowers are in full bloom. A memorial stone on the northwest wall commemorates the battle of 1835 that drove the Ottomans out of the village. *O4*

INSIDER TIP
Breathtaking views

9 PLAVNICA

An ultra-modern hotel complex *(Plavnica Eco Resort tel. 020 44 37 00 | plavnica.me)* has been built in the village of Plavnica on the north bank of Lake Skadar. The resort includes two restaurants: the sophisticated *Plavnica (€€–€€€)* and the *Rotonda (€–€€)*, which is an easy-going place with a beer hall and pizzeria. From the futuristic terrace, hotel guests have a view across the large swimming pool to the lake. The resort is also an events venue: concerts, fashion shows and beauty contests are held here. ▢ P4

SPORT & ACTIVITIES

Hikers and cyclists can follow the 3.5km-long *art tour*: a series of works by Montenegrin sculptors on the millers' path between the villages of Poseljani and Smokovci. You can extend the tour as far as Rijeka Crnojevića. There is also a *wine route* between Virpazar and Rijeka. Anglers and bird lovers can explore the lake by boat. Operators in Virpazar also offer boat trips for tourists.

The visitor centres in Vranjina, Murići and Rijeka Crnojevića provide local information. The centre in Virpazar also rents hiking equipment.

PODGORICA

(▢ O2) **In the early evening at the very latest, it will become clear where the heartbeat of the capital city (pop. 200,000) can be felt: from 5pm all cars are banned from the zone between Freedom Street (Slobode) and Marka Miljanova.**

After that, the area near the Parliament and National Theatre belongs to those who are out for a stroll. And anyone who stays here longer, and is not just passing through, will soon learn to take a closer look: Podgorica may not be among the

Like London, Podgorica has its own Millennium Bridge

most beautiful of Europe's capital cities and may well be lacking in major sights, but the generous public parks and lively shopping streets make this small capital worth a visit. Two rivers, the Morača and Ribnica, flow through the middle of the city and four others have their courses not far away – this is why it was originally called Ribnica (*ribe* means fish) before being renamed Podgorica ("at the foot of the hill") in 1326. During Yugoslavia's Socialist period, the city in the fertile Zeta Valley was given the name of Titograd in honour of the special commitment of Montenegrin partisans before finally reverting to its old name in 1992. In 2017, the foundation stone for a synagogue was laid although building work has not yet started.

SIGHTSEEING

OLD TOWN (STARA VAROŠ)

This is a classic, cosy old town, and a stroll through the simple and partly dilapidated but also charming and authentic alleyways is fascinating.

The Ribnica river forms the boundary between the new *(nova)* and old *(stara)* sections of town. The days of Ottoman rule come back to life when you hear the Muezzin calling the faithful to prayer in the Stara Varoš quarter. The clock tower from the 17th century, *Sahat kula*, is one of the few well-preserved examples of Islamic architecture in Podgorica. It is on *Trg Bećir Bega Osmanagića.*

GALERIJA CENTAR ★ ☆

The Montenegrin Centre for Contemporary Art gives a good overview of art from the 20th and 21st centuries. The largest section of the collection is on display in the old winter palace of King Nikola in the Kruševac park on the Morača river where the Gallery of the Non-aligned States was housed until 1985. And even today, paintings from Montenegro and the other republics of former Yugoslavia still hang on the walls alongside works by artists from Bolivia, Egypt and Cuba. The park at the rear is also beautiful. *At the time of this guide going to print, the gallery was closed for renovation work | Kruševac bb | csucg.me | admission free | ☉ 1 hr*

SABORNI HRAM HRISTOVOG VASKRSENJA

Consecrated in 2013 and already a landmark of the capital, the

---

WHERE TO START?

Trg Republike: this square is right in the modern city centre on Slobode Street, and from the airport it is a 15-minute car journey. All around you'll find shops and shopping malls as well as plenty of parking spaces. The Bulevar Svetog Petra Cetinjskog with its magnificent public parks is only a few minutes' walk away. And then it's another 400m to reach the Ottoman clock tower of Sahat kula in the historic old town.

Serbian-Orthodox Cathedral of the Resurrection of Christ with its almost 36m-high dome and the deliberately aged stone façade is Montenegro's biggest Orthodox church. Buildings don't have to be ancient to be worth a visit! *Bulevar Džordža Vašingtona 3*

GORICA

From this quarter on the northern hill there is a fantastic view of the Morača with the Millennium Bridge and the stadium of the FK Budućnost Podgorica football club. You will also be able to take a look inside the 12th-century church *Sv. Đorđe* (Saint George). Gorica is directly above the so-called new town *(Novi Grad)* in the centre of the capital.

EATING & DRINKING

BERLIN

There are many modern restaurants, particularly in Njegoševa Street, and some of them even have a hipster flair. The Berlin serves beer and a few hearty dishes at low prices. Night owls will love the fact that the restaurant is open daily until late. *Njegoševa 24 | tel. 020 23 43 67 | short.travel/ mon12 | €*

KONOBA LANTERNA

Really cosy: in an old house with mighty stone walls you can relax in a rustic ambience and feast on gener-ous servings of hearty food. Friendly, quick service and low prices. Good beer and house wines as well as frequent live music create a lively atmos-phere. Ask the waiter

INSIDER TIP
Fresh cheese

for fresh, regional village cheese as a starter or dessert. A great breakfast is served from Monday to Saturday. *Marka Miljanova 41 | tel. 020 66 31 63 | €–€€*

MASALA ART

Indian cuisine in the Balkans? Why not? A great selection of authentic dishes, and you can tell that an enthu-siastic Indian family runs this restaurant. Fair prices, and easy to reach in the city centre's new town *(Novi Grad). Vasa Raičkovića 13a | tel. 020 24 26 65 | masalaart.me | €–€€*

SHOPPING

SHOPPING MALLS 🐖

If you are interested in a bargain on international brands, visit one of the big shopping malls of Podgorica such as *Delta City (Cetinjski put | deltacity. me)* or *Mall of Montenegro (Bulevar Save Kovačevića 74 | mallofmonte negro.com)*. Summer sales run from June to August.

SPORT & ACTIVITIES

KONJIČKI KLUB PONY 🐎

This pony club is on the northwesterly outskirts of the city. Here you and your children can take riding lessons or simply ride on one of the horses. If riding is not your thing, the grounds include a nice petting zoo with ponies, goats, deer, rabbits, donkeys, chickens, etc. Plus there's a playground and var-ious snack stalls. *Vranići bb | tel. 068 71 94 04 | FB: Konjički klub Pony*

NIGHTLIFE

Once the heat of the day has passed, life returns to the streets between Stanka Dragojevića, Karađorđeva, Slobode and Hercegovačka, where you will find most of Podgorica's bars and pubs. There is something for everybody: the *Velvet Nocni Klub (Bokeška 24 | FB: velvet.podgorica)*, the hip *Buda-Bar (Bulevar Stanka Dragojevića 26 | FB: Budabarpg)*, the *Scottish Pub McCloud (Hercegovačka 3 | FB)* or the *Zeppelin Lounge Bar & Pub (Njegoševa 46 | FB: zeppelinmne)*.

The ☂ *Kino Kultura* cinema *(V Proleterske Brigade 1)* shows mainly foreign films in English with Serbian subtitles.

AROUND PODGORICA

Taste the wine right where it ripens

🔟 ŠIPČANIK

10km/10 mins from Podgorica on the E762

The best wines of Montenegro are grown south of the capital, on the 2,300-hectare Čamovsko polje. The wine estate Plantaže has a giant-size wine cellar 30m below ground that is open to visitors. You can also take a tour of the vineyards: a miniature train transports you across the plain among millions of vines. Alongside the local Vranac (red) and Krstač (white) varieties, some excellent Sauvignon, Chardonnay or Cabernet grapes ripen in Montenegro's sunshine. *Wine tasting 12–31 euros, more expensive premium tours/tastings incl. lunch or dinner in the wine cellar restaurant. Guided tours for individuals and groups also available | plantaze.com |* 📖 *P3*

1️⃣1️⃣ DUKLIJA

5km/10 mins from the centre of Podgorica

The first Illyrian city conquered by the Romans is just north of Podgorica, near the village of Rogami. The ruins include traces of an ancient sewage system along with the stone remains of baths and a basilica. 📖 *O2*

THE
NORTHWEST

Montenegro, a country that feels quite gentle on the coast, shows off its wild side in the Durmitor Mountains and the Tara Canyon. There are more than 20 mountain peaks over 2,000m high, more than a dozen glacial lakes, and countless springs, brooks and rivers. To experience the pristine beauty of this region, visit the area between Žabljak and Nikšić.

The Durmitor National Park offers mountaineers a wide selection of routes and, in winter, the ski slopes provide some of the best

The Đurđevića Tara Bridge towers above the abyss

downhill runs on the Balkan Peninsula. A rafting trip on the Tara, the wild river of the north, has become something of a must for all visitors to Montenegro.

A feast for the eyes at any time of the year is the Black Lake *(Crno jezero)* near Žabljak and the Ledena pećina ice cave with its stalactites and stalagmites. However, even if hiking and rafting are not your thing, the views alone into the incredibly steep Tara Canyon are worth the journey.

THE NORTHWEST

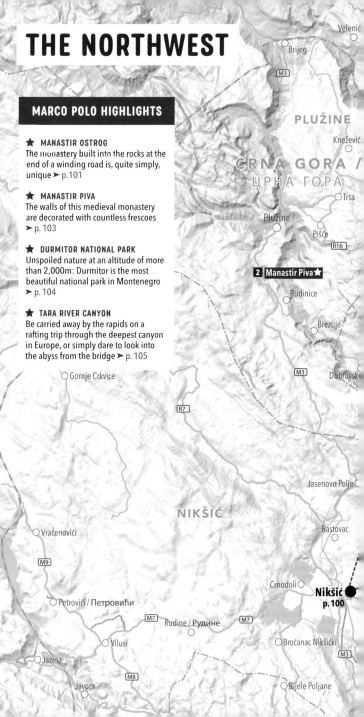

MARCO POLO HIGHLIGHTS

★ MANASTIR OSTROG
The monastery built into the rocks at the end of a winding road is, quite simply, unique ➤ p.101

★ MANASTIR PIVA
The walls of this medieval monastery are decorated with countless frescoes ➤ p. 103

★ DURMITOR NATIONAL PARK
Unspoiled nature at an altitude of more than 2,000m: Durmitor is the most beautiful national park in Montenegro ➤ p. 104

★ TARA RIVER CANYON
Be carried away by the rapids on a rafting trip through the deepest canyon in Europe, or simply dare to look into the abyss from the bridge ➤ p. 105

Velenić

Brijeg

M3

PLUŽINE

Kneževič

CRNA GORA /
ЦРНА ГОРА

Trsa

Plužine

Pišče

R16

2 Manastir Piva ★

Rudinice

Brezuje

M3 Dubrovsk

R7

Gornje Crkvice

Jasenovo Polje

NIKŠIĆ

Rastovac

Vraćenovići

M9

Crnodoli

Nikšić
p. 100

Petrovići / Петровићи

M7 Rudine / Рудине M7

Broćanac Nikšićki

Vilusi

M3

Jazina

M8

Javora

Bijele Poljane

Podkukanj

R18

6 Pljevlja

ЦЕНТРАЛНА
СРБИЈА

Otilovići

Zabrde

M6

Odžak

Gačević

R11

PLJEVLJA

Mijakovići

Marina Šuma

Kosanica

Durmitor National Park ★

25km, 30 mins

Đurđevića Tara

3

Žabljak
p. 102

M6

5 Tara River Canyon ★

4

Durmitor-
Ring

Njegovuđa

ŽABLJAK

Pašina voda

R10

Gornja Dobrilovina

75km, 1 hr 20 mins

M6

Gornja Bukovica

R20

Slatina

Donja Bukovica

Bistrica

ŠAVNIK

MOJKOVAC

Šavnik

Tušinja

Krnja Jela

M6

R21

Moračko Trebaljevo

Dragovića Polje

Kolašin

Ivanje

KOLAŠIN

Seoca

Crkvine

25km, 40 mins

Gračanica

Liverovići

Tara

Međuriječje

Uvač

7.5 km
4.66 mi

1 Manastir Ostrog ★

Ostrog Monastery clings to the rock face like an eagle's nest

NIKŠIĆ

(📖 U13) **The second largest city in Montenegro (pop. 72,000) has always been overshadowed historically by Podgorica and Cetinje.**

However, it's a city with a palace, a fortress, an important church, and with great destinations in the immediate surroundings – especially Ostrog Monastery.

Although Nikšić was known as "the city of steel and beer" during the Tito era, not much remained of the steel industry after the Yugoslavian wars, and hardly anybody drank the famous *Nikšićko pivo* that had been brewed here since 1896; in fact, it was not until the state-run brewery was sold that things started to look up and the unemployment rate fell.

SIGHTSEEING

ZAVIČAJNI MUZEJ GRADA NIKŠIĆA

The local heritage museum is housed in the former palace of King Nikola. The two floors of exhibits from the 18th and 19th centuries – and especially from the reign of King Nikola – bring the past back to life. *Mon–Sat 8am–8pm, Sun 8am–1pm; Oct–March Mon–Sat 8am–3pm, Sun 8am–1pm | Trg Šaka Petrovića 1 | muzejniksic.me | admission 2 euros | ⊙ 1 hr*

SV. VASILIJE OSTROŠKI

St Vasilije Church, which was consecrated in 1900, is located next to the Royal Palace. It was erected in honour of the soldiers from the area who fell in the battle against the Ottomans in 1878. *Trg Šaka Petrovića*

UTVRĐENJE 🐄

The approximately 200m-long, well-preserved fortress at the western entrance to *Nikšić* was erected by the Ottoman rulers in the 16th century. From June to September it is used as an open-air stage for music and theatre. *Admission free*

EATING & DRINKING

There are many small pubs and bistros in the centre of town, and a few good restaurants can be found in hotels, such as the *Trim* and *Trebjesa*.

FOREST CAFÉ & LOUNGE BAR

Modern interior and excellent cuisine – the café, a local branch of a wine bar in Podgorica, is popular in *Nikšić*, especially for the Balkan specialities such as *ćevapčići* (grilled minced meat) and *pljeskavica* (a type of spiced hamburger). They even serve craft beer. *Ivana Milutinovića | tel. 040 21 37 66 | FB: forestniksic | €–€€*

MANITOVAC 🎪

This café-restaurant with a thatched roof, wooden beams, a terrace and a relaxed and friendly atmosphere is great for a stop-over. They have a big play lawn for children near the riverbank and serve classic hearty dishes and delicious desserts. *Hercegovački put | mobile 067 32 14 32 | manitovac.me | €€*

AROUND NIKŠIĆ

1 MANASTIR OSTROG ★ 🐄

25km/40 mins from Nikšić on the E762 and local roads

At first glance, the walls of the small room where the body of St Vasilije is preserved look as if they are covered in tattoos. In fact, frescoes of the saints have been painted directly onto the stone as one last sign of respect for the builder of the monastery. In 1665, the then Metropolitan (Orthodox bishop with authority over the bishops of a province) of Herzegovina, Vasilije Ostrovski, had the white building hewn into the rock after he had fled from the Ottomans and been forced to abandon his ancestral seat further to the west. Later the sanctuary became a place of pilgrimage for believers from all parts of the former Yugoslavia. Many Orthodox families still have their children christened here. Catholics and Muslims also consider the place holy. *Daily 6am–8pm | admission free, donations welcome | ⏱ 2 hrs*

Please note that the road up to Ostrog is steep and winding! First you get to the lower monastery and from there you continue uphill to the upper monastery which perches spectacularly in the rock face. From the car park it is another 10 minutes on foot. There is also a lovely half-hour walk via steps from the lower to the upper monastery.

The *Koliba Bogetići* restaurant *(mobile 067 88 81 89 | koliba.me | €–€€)*, 8km south on the road towards

Podgorica, serves excellent traditional food. The service is

INSIDER TIP
Fresh mountain air

friendly and the fresh air invigorating. The owners are proud to serve generous portions at low prices using fresh local produce. *U13*

ŽABLJAK

(V12) **At 1,450m, Žabljak is the highest town in Montenegro as well as being a centre of mountain tourism and winter sports – with many ideal excursion destinations in the immediate vicinity.**

Although Žabljak was destroyed during World War II, the typical mountain houses with their steep roofs still make this small community (pop. 2,000) a charming place to visit. But when the early-morning mist rises from the Black Lake and disappears among the peaks of the Bobotov kuk and the other mountains (over 2,000m high), it is hard to believe that people have ever set foot here.

EATING & DRINKING

CAFFE CLUB CUDNA SUMA
A cosy restaurant in the town centre, designed with lots of old wood and open from 8am until after midnight. A great atmosphere without unnecessary hype. Whether you come for breakfast, lunch (tortillas are delicious) or evening drinks, you will always be in the right place. *Vuka Karadžića | tel. 067 78 77 77 | €€*

KRCMA NOSTALGIJA
The name "nostalgic country inn" basically says it all: no gourmet cuisine, but typical hearty Montenegrin food, including several vegetarian options, in a cosy atmosphere. There are also some outdoor tables. *Vuka Karadžića | mobile 069 63 06 96 | €-€€*

RESTAURANT OR'O
This restaurant with its big, beautiful terrace is a great meeting place after rafting, hiking or a long day on the slopes. A comfortable place to wait for your food with a freshly pulled beer. The speciality is Montenegrin lamb, but there are vegetarian options as well on the short menu. Breakfast is also great. *Njegoševa | mobile 069 40 62 10 | FB: restoranoro | €€*

SHOPPING

AROMA CENTAR
This not-so-small mall (2,100m²), arguably the best place for shopping in the town, includes a supermarket and a number of small shops. You may want to buy some souvenirs in the form of sheep's milk cheese, spirits or clothes. The café is open until late at night. *Narodnih Heroja*

SPORT & ACTIVITIES

In winter the ski resorts near Žabljak are a major attraction. There are seven available lifts with a total length of 3,900m, and a day pass costs approximately 15 euros. In summer you can book rafting tours, jeep safaris, mountain biking, canyoning excursions and

Adventurous riding holidays near Žabljak

book rafting tours, jeep safaris, mountain biking, canyoning excursions and paragliding, as well as horse riding and angling trips, hikes or eco-tours. The majestic, unspoiled natural landscape of the northwest is unique and conditions for all these activities are ideal. There is a wide choice of tour operators and most work with exceptional local guides who have expert knowledge of the region. The prices are comparable. *Eco-Tours (Dunje Đokić | mobile 067 25 90 20 | eco-tours.co.me)* has its offices in Kolašin in the northeast, but also has the best offers for the northwestern region of the country.

AROUND ŽABLJAK

2 MANASTIR PIVA ★

Approx. 60km/1 hr from Žabljak on the P14

This monastery has a chequered history: in order to prevent the 16th-century three-nave church falling victim to the dam being constructed in Plužine, people began dismantling it bit by bit and rebuilding it at its current location in 1969. This operation took just as long as the initial construction of the church. The walls are decorated with frescoes, which cover an area of more than 1,000m². Pay particular attention to the fresco over the south entrance: unique in Orthodox churches, it shows a picture of the Turkish Pasha Mehmed Sokolović, a relative of the Serbian patriarch at the time who had converted to Islam. *Generally accessible all day | ⏱ 1 hr | 🗺 U12*

🄳 DURMITOR NATIONAL PARK ★

2.5km/5 mins from Žabljak to the information centre at the Black Lake

In 1980 Durmitor National Park was declared a UNESCO World Heritage Site. Its area of 390km² offers all that any nature lover could desire: deep canyons, high mountains, caves, glacial lakes and a boundless variety of flora and fauna. The area around Žabljak alone has around 1,300 plant species and it is also a paradise for bird lovers.

The park extends over a high plateau at an altitude of around 1,500m with peaks that are even higher – the highest is the Bobotov kuk at 2,522m. Climbers have five huts at their disposal as well as accommodation options in *Škarka, Šusica*, at the *Sedlo* mountain saddle and some limited possibilities in *Lokvice* and *Velika Kalica*. You can spend the night in cosy peasant huts at the *Black Lake (Crno jezero)* in summer and winter and rent private rooms locally. The *national park information centre (Ul. Jovana Cvijića | Žabljak | tel. 052 36 02 28 | npdurmitor@nparkovi.me)* can provide further information.

There is a demanding hike from Žabljak to the Bobotov kuk that takes around seven hours. The path begins 3km outside of the village at Crno jezero, where a signpost indicates the marked route to *Indjini Dolovi*. After approximately four hours of hiking through karst craters and scree, you arrive at the *Ledena pećina (ice cave)* at an altitude of more than 2,000m. There is a further steep path up to the *Velika Previja* viewpoint where you can also catch your breath at a spring. After that, it is only another 45 minutes to the peak of the Bobotov kuk. You make the downward hike from Velika Previja via *Zeleni Vir* and *Urdeni Do* to *Dobri Do* or the mountaineers' shelter in *Sedlo*.

A tip for those who don't want to overdo the hiking: there is a lovely hiking trail round the Black Lake which is easily managed in one or two hours. *Park admission 3 euros | 🗺 U–W 11–12*

INSIDER TIP
Take it easy

4 DURMITOR RING

76km/3 hrs, start/finish in Žabljak

A fantastic scenic road, signposted as Panorama Circular Road No. 2, Durmitor Ring starts and finishes in Žabljak. Initially you follow road P5 southbound and then turn off onto the P14. Soon you reach one spectacular viewpoint after another, passing the country's highest peak, *Bobotov kuk*. Park the car to make your ascent to the summit on a hike covering a 900-m height difference.

Later on, the circular road becomes gentler and less steep, before winding itself once again into tight bends. The last 20km before returning to Žabljak have more fabulous views as you approach the gigantic Tara Canyon. Approx. 10km before Žabljak you reach an incredible viewpoint *(GPS coordinates: 43.188214, 19.061746)* over the deep gorge.

Overall, the road is often twisty with many bends and climbs, but it tar-macked throughout. With a bit of luck, you will find passing places, but it is advisable not to attempt the route in large vehicles such as motorhomes. *U–V 12*

5 TARA RIVER CANYON ★

Approx. 20km/30 mins from Žabljak, on the P5 to Đurđevića Tara Bridge

This is not only the longest river in the country, it is also the most beautiful: the Tara winds its way for 158km through the Montenegrin landscape, cutting through rocks and, shortly after Leveri, plunging 1,300m down a dozen cascades. The river has created the deepest canyon in Europe and – after the Grand Canyon – the second deepest in the world; reason enough for UNESCO to

Hike the trail to the high mountain pasture at Sedlo peak in the Durmitor National Park

An unforgettable adventure at 170m: take the zip-line across the Tara River Canyon

declare the Tara a World Heritage Site in 1977. This wild river, which the Montenegrins have christened the "Tear of Europe", flows so slowly near the town of Bistrica that you can even wade across it. This place has been nicknamed the "Devil's Lies" because the locals claim that it is possible to leap from one side to the other with a single jump.

The Montenegrins believe that everyone should journey down the Tara – in a kayak, boat or on an inflatable raft – at least once in a lifetime (see p. 34). The view from high up is also spectacular. In 1941, engineer Lazar Janković designed the 🐖 Đurđevića Tara Bridge 150m above the river. Just one year later, he blew up the central arch in an attempt to prevent the advance of Nazi troops. Snack booths and a memorial invite visitors to make

a stop for a rest, and it is a unique opportunity with dizzying views to walk across the bridge and back.

At the bridge, 🎭 Durmitor Adventure (May–Sept daily, April, Oct weather-permitting | mobile 069 89 33 15 | durmitoradventure.com | 10 euros/person) offers a breathtaking ride, also for teenagers: hang on tight to the zip-line and fly across the canyon at a speed of up to 50kmh.

At the end of the zip-line is a campsite with a restaurant. This is the starting point for great rafting tours organised by the same operator (book in advance). The "half-day tour" (dur mitoradventure.com | 45 euros/pers | ⏱ 2 hrs) is absolutely sufficient. Wearing wetsuits and rubber shoes, you experience the River Tara in inflatable boats. Highlights include a wild

6 PLJEVLJA

60km/1 hr from Žabljak on the P4

Few foreign tourists make it to Pljevlja (pop. 19,000), Montenegro's most northwesterly city. However, the trip is really worthwhile. You can admire the town's landmark – the *Hussein Pasha Mosque (Husein pašina džamija)*, with its tall slender minaret, erected shortly after the Ottoman conquest in the 16th century – and also explore the traces of ancient Illyrian and Roman settlements in the vicinity. Archaeologists found the remains of a Roman town near the hamlet of *Komine* but were only able to decipher the first letter of its name. The site is now known as *Municipio S*. Finds from the Iron Age were uncovered in *Gotovuša*. And don't forget to visit the monks in the early 16th-century Trinity Monastery (Manastir Sv. Trojica) in the centre of Pljevlja. They have one of the richest collections of icons, historical documents and books on the entire Balkan Peninsula *(generally accessible all day | ⏱ 1 hr)*.

INSIDER TIP **Icons galore**

You can eat well in the *Taša restaurant (mobile 069 57 01 77 | restorantasa.me | €–€€)* where they serve typical dishes at fair prices and in a friendly ambience. Menu in English available. 📖 *V11*

waterfall and passing underneath the Tara Bridge. Your good-natured guide will steer the boat and its international crew skilfully through a few challenging rapids. In difficult spots you will need to help with the paddling, which is quite manageable for both the young and the old. The reward at the finish line is a light lunch.

If you need a break from so much adventure, we recommend the restaurant of the small *Motel Tara MB (Đurđevića Tara bb | mobile 069 99 37 73 | mbturist.com | €€)* where you can either have a proper meal or just order a cup of coffee. The terrace has excellent views of the spectacular Tara Bridge, and from the motel's car park you can walk across the bridge. 📖 *v12*

INSIDER TIP **Convenient parking**

THE
NORTHEAST

WILD & UNSPOILT

Mountains over 2,000m high with snow-capped peaks well into summer, deep valleys, crystal-clear rivers and shimmering blue lakes: there is a surprise round every corner here, where four countries – Serbia, Albania, Kosovo and Montenegro – come together.

Those in search of peace and quiet will find it here in the fresh alpine air. And that goes for any time of the year and whether you are on one of the numerous hiking trails through the Bjelasica

Glacial lakes, such as the Biogradsko jezero, are known as "Eyes of the Mountains"

Mountains, along the Mrtvica and Morača canyons, or skiing downhill from Mount Ćupović.

There is even more to discover: hidden away in the northeastern highlands between Kolašin, Bijelo Polje and Berane is the Biogradska gora National Park, with one of the last primeval forests in Europe. And in the centre is Biogradsko jezero, the enchanted glacial lake that gave the national park its name, where the mirrored reflection of the sky shimmers on its calm waters.

THE NORTHEAST

○ Ujniče

○ Tomaševo

Bijelo Polje
p. 112

Crvena Lokva

R11

Prošćenje

Crna Poda ○

MOJKOVAC

Brezovac ○

M2

Gojakovići ○

R10

Ravna Rijeka

Polja

Mojkovac

CRNA GORA /
ЦРНА ГОРА

50km, 1 hr

Sjerogošte

3 Biogradska gora National Park ★

M2

25km, 30 mins

○ Gornje Lipovo

Lubnice ○

KOLAŠIN

Kolašin
p. 114

○ Seoca

M2

○ Vranještica

ANDRIJEVICA

4 Manastir Morača ★

Mateševo ○

Trešnjevik

Jabuka ○

Bare Kraljske

R19

70km, 1¾ hrs

Kralje

○ Uvač

MARCO POLO HIGHLIGHTS

★ **BIOGRADSKA GORA NATIONAL PARK**
Primeval forests and glacial lakes invite
you to unwind ➤ p. 115

★ **MANASTIR MORAČA**
The magnificent frescoes in this monastery
bear witness to the influence of the
Serbian Orthodox Church in the Middle
Ages ➤ p. 116

★ **PLAV**
A delightful contrast near the Albanian
border: 18th-century mosques and an
alpine lake surrounded by mountains that
tower over 2,000m ➤ p.117

BIJELO POLJE

(▥ W12) **This town (pop. 16,000) is just 20km from the Serbian border. Its name means "white field" after the splendid mass of wild flowers that adorn Bijelo Polje every year in spring.**

However, the skiing region in the Bjelasica Mountains is only a short distance away and the hilly landscape around the town is also completely white in winter.

Founded in the 12th century, Bijelo Polje soon developed into a cultural and religious centre. It is situated on the banks of the third-longest river in Montenegro, the Lim, that flows northwards towards Serbia. The town, which is surrounded by countless springs, became a bishop's seat in 1321 but came under Ottoman control shortly thereafter. Today, thanks to its tourist infrastructure, it is predominantly known as a great base for adventurers in Montenegro's exciting northeast.

SIGHTSEEING

SV. PETAR

One of the most important Orthodox manuscripts was created in the ancient St Peter's Church at the end of the 12th century: the so-called *Miroslav Gospel*. A copy of the document is on display in the nave of the church while – much to the annoyance of the locals – the original is kept in the Serbian capital Belgrade. The whitewashed church tower was once

The Bjelasica Mountains are a paradise for skiers and snowboarders

used as a minaret: after the Ottomans conquered the city, they converted the church into a mosque and members of the Christian faith were not able to worship in it again until 1912. *Crkva*

SV. NIKOLA

The unassuming St Nicholas's Church on the bank of the River Lim has a library from the 14th century where dozens of valuable manuscripts and early printed books are housed. The frescoes and icons are equally remarkable. *Nedeljka Merdovića*

EATING & DRINKING

There are restaurants and cafés in the centre of the small town. Most offer "continental cuisine" with a lot of meat and few vegetables. The prices are fairly reasonable wherever you eat.

RESTORAN KARAVAN

This motel restaurant is in the suburbs, on the main road 10km north of the centre of Bijelo Polje, but with a great view of the River Lim from the spacious terrace. Specialities include oven-roasted lamb and goat. *Mobile 068 13 75 61 | €–€€*

SUGAR RESTO CAFE ⚑

A friendly, modern and uncomplicated restaurant where you can choose the ingredients for your sandwich. They also serve good coffee and wonderful cakes. Outside there are nice seats in a small pedestrian zone. *Slobode | sugar-caffe.business. site*

AROUND BIJELO POLJE

1 ROŽAJE

64km/1 hr from Bijelo Polje

The small towns in the area around Bijelo Polje, such as *Rožaje* (pop. 9,000), have also developed into centres of tourism. You can ski here in winter and nature lovers and sports enthusiasts will also find plenty of activities to keep themselves busy in summer. The *tourism office in Rožaje (tel. 051 27 01 58)* provides information. 🔲 *X13*

2 BERANE

35km/40 mins from Bijelo Polje on the E763 and E65

In Tito's Yugoslavia, Berane (pop. 12,000) was renamed Ivangrad after a heroic son of the city, Ivan Milutinović, who fought as a partisan against the Germans in World War II. The sleepy backwater flourished under Tito: factories were built and the people had work. However, when Yugoslavia disintegrated, this prosperity disappeared along with the name.

But that does not detract from the idyllic location; the small town (at an altitude of almost 700m) on the banks of the River Lim is surrounded by mountains. Thanks to favourable wind conditions the city has recently become a hot spot for paragliders. The well-preserved 13th-century monastery of *Đurđevi stupovi (generally accessible all day | ⏱ 1 hr)* is not far away.

The town has a few good restaurants, especially the *Dva Jelena (Svetosavska | mobile 068 52 42 16 | €)* with particularly friendly staff and a relaxed atmosphere. Although the restaurant's name translates as "Two Stags", you simply must try their exquisite chicken in a wine sauce. ▭ *X13*

INSIDER TIP
Delicious chicken

KOLAŠIN

(▭ W13) **This, the most important winter sports town (pop. 3,000) in the northeast of Montenegro, lies at an altitude of 960m. It is also the country's water divide.**

While the Tara flows towards the Drina and then to the Black Sea by way of the Danube, the Morača's course is towards the Adriatic. Its proximity to the Bjelasica ski area and Biogradska gora National Park makes Kolašin an ideal starting point to discover all the northeast has to offer.

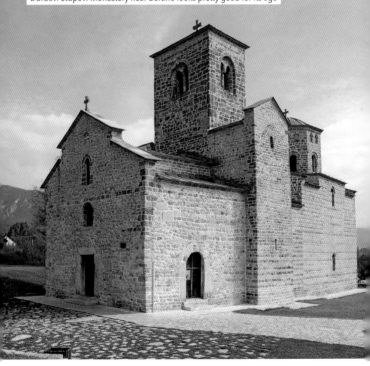
Đurđevi Stupovi Monastery near Berane looks pretty good for its age

SIGHTSEEING

BOTANIČKA BAŠTA DULOVINE 🕴

This "Botanical Garden" is really the small private garden of charming Mrs Zora Marjanović-Vincek and her husband who are more than happy to open it up for you and give you a full guided tour. The two plant lovers have collected more than 400 species in a tight space, the majority being medicinal herbs. Feel free to immerse yourself in the aromatic scent and to even taste a few of them. *Dulovina, Put Braće Vujisic* | ☉ *1 hr*

EATING & DRINKING

GORŠTAK PUB

This restaurant in the town centre is a good place to be at any time of day because, apart from hearty food such as home-made burgers, they serve freshly pulled draught beer until late in the evening. You can also enjoy breakfast from 7am or just have a coffee break. *IV. Proleterske 1 | mobile 067 07 13 80 | Instagram: gorstak. pub | €*

KONOBA 🐷

Here you can enjoy traditional dishes at fair prices in a small and rustic house made of wood and stone: it's great fun! There is a restricted menu during low season. *IV. Proleterske | mobile 069 60 91 44 | €*

SAVARDAK

The name says it all: *Savardak* are the pyramid-like highland huts, and the restaurant (on the way out of town towards the Bjelasica ski centre) is housed in one of them. The menu consists of hearty grilled food. You should definitely try the cheesy Montenegrin polenta *kačamak* or the wheat stew *cicvara*! *Biocinovići | mobile 069 05 12 64 | €–€€*

SPORT & ACTIVITIES

The nearby winter sport resorts of *Kolašin 1450* and *Kolašin 1600* (*kolasin.me*) at altitudes of 1,450m up to above 2,000m offer much skiing fun, with a ski pass costing approx. 20 euros.

The area around Kolašin and the national park also have a lot to offer in summer from hiking and biking to riding, rafting, tubing and even jeep safaris. All of these activities can be booked at the *Tourist Agency Sport Turist* whose young staff are not just friendly and professional but also speak English (*Junaka Mojkovačke Bitke | mobile 068 00 30 56 | sport turist.me*).

> **INSIDER TIP**
> For active holiday-makers

AROUND KOLAŠIN

🔳 BIOGRADSKA GORA NATIONAL PARK ⭐

25km/30 mins from Kolašin on the E65 and the mountain road to the lake shore

One of the last primeval forests in

Europe is within the nature reserve that was declared a national park in 1952. Preserving so much unspoiled nature in such a small area is not least thanks to Prince Nikola I. As early as 1878, only six years after Yellowstone National Park was established in the USA, he proclaimed Biogradska gora an environmentally protected area. Today, the park has about 2,000 types of plants and over 200 bird species. The lakes here, which are known as "eyes of the mountain" *(gorske oči)* are particularly interesting. The loveliest is *Lake Biogradsko (Biogradsko jezero). Eco-Tours (Dunje Đokić | Kolašin | mobile 067 25 90 20 | eco-tours. co.me)* have a wide variety of activities on offer including hiking, cycling, horse riding or jeep tours in the park. The choice is yours. A recommendation for a two-day hike from Kolašin is given on p. 122 of this guide. *W12–13*

4 MANASTIR MORAČA ★

25km/30 mins from Kolašin on the E65

Morača Monastery, built in 1252, is one of the most important Serbian Orthodox monasteries – both historically and artistically. It lies southwest of Kolašin, just after the confluence of the Mrtvica and Morača rivers. The frescoes that were painted in the 16th and 17th centuries, after the church had been plundered by the Ottomans, make a visit particularly worthwhile. Compared to most other monasteries in the country, this one is particularly well preserved and maintained with pretty buildings that are really worth seeing. The entire complex has an unusually tranquil and peaceful atmosphere. *Daily 8am–6pm | V13*

ORTHODOX CHURCH

There are numerous Orthodox medieval churches, monasteries and chapels in the north of Montenegro; many of them are decorated with magnificent frescoes and icons. They are among the sacred sites of the Orthodox faith, the exegesis of Christianity that was promoted after the division of the Roman Empire. In the Middle Ages the churches were places of sanctuary in the battle against the Ottomans.

The Montenegrin Orthodox Church lost its independence when the country became part of Yugoslavia in 1918. In Socialist Yugoslavia, religion was not encouraged and the churches remained empty.

In 1993, the Montenegrin Orthodox Church again split from its Serbian Orthodox brothers in Belgrade. Since then, the two religious communities have been in dispute with no resolution in sight. Today, three out of four Montenegrins describe themselves as Orthodox Christians.

The beautiful national park around Lake Biogradsko is home to countless butterflies

5 PLAV ★

70km from Kolašin, 1¾ hrs by car on the windy but modern M9

The *Vezirova Mosque* from 1741 and the *Redžepagića Mosque*, which was built three decades later, are the main architectural highlights of Plav (pop. 3,600). The *Kula Redžepagića* defensive tower of the former ruling family is just up the hill from the mosque.

The mountain lake *Plavsko jezero* is tucked away in the dense forests close to the town. It lies at the foot of Mount Prokletije (2,700m), which is known among locals as the "cursed mountain" because of its steep, bare rock faces. Plav is an excellent starting point for cross-border trekking tours in Montenegro, Albania and Kosovo.

The transnational 'Peaks of the Balkans Trail' is a demanding hike into the Prokletije region, one of the most isolated mountain areas in the western Balkans. The tour passes through spectacular landscapes and barren mountain ranges and past secluded lakes, waterfalls, alpine pastures full of flowers and picturesque mountain villages. It forms a circular route of 192km and takes around ten days accompanied by experienced mountain guides. Mountaineering experience is absolutely essential. Visit *peaksofthebalkans.com*. ⌂ X14

INSIDER TIP
The ultimate mountain tour

DISCOVERY TOURS

Do you want to get under the skin of the country? Then these discovery tours provide the perfect guide. They include advice on which sights to visit, tips on where to stop for that perfect holiday snap, a choice of the best places to eat and drink and suggestions for fun activities.

❶ FROM THE COAST TO THE ROCKY CLIFFS AND BACK

➤ Travel into the country's interior on old, winding roads
➤ Jump into deep blue-water coves
➤ Treat yourself to a cocktail on the beach

📍	Tivat	🏁	Tivat
🔄	Approx. 230km	🚗	2 days (7½ hrs total driving time)

DAY 1
❶ Tivat

FROM A SUBMARINE TO THE CATHEDRAL

The tour begins in ❶ Tivat ➤ p. 57 where, in an unusual visit, you can feel the squeeze inside the

118

A stroll through Kotor's charming old town

ex-submarine of the Yugoslavian Navy in front of the Museum Arsenal. *On the E80 drive north to Lepetane and, via Prčanj, to* ❷ Kotor ➤ p. 50. Here, you can watch the big cruise ships from the promenade, as they navigate through the fjord. Walk through the medieval old town to St Tryphon's Cathedral.

WIND YOUR WAY UPHILL

When you head south out of Kotor, you reach a cross-roads after about 4km. Turn left onto the R1 and head uphill in the direction of Cetinje. This is the start of the ❸ Ladder of Cattaro, which was, until the end of the 19th century, the only access route to the interior of the country. *The road winds its way uphill* and offers breath-taking panoramas of the Bay of Kotor; the most impressive view is *shortly before the village of Krstač.* Soon you arrive at Njeguši ➤ p. 87, which is famous not only for being the birthplace of the poet Prince Njegoš, but also for its delicious smoked ham and hard cheese. Try the specialities at ❹ Kod Pera Na Bukovicu ➤ p. 87.

After Njeguši, *the R1 continues uphill* and the sparse mountain landscape is revealed in all its glory. In the

17km 20 mins

❷ **Kotor**

11km 15 mins

❸ **Ladder of Cattaro**

18km 20 mins

❹ **Kod Pera Na Bukovicu**

14km 15 mins

❺ Cetinje

22km 25 mins

❻ Njegoš Mausoleum

57km 1 hr

❼ Jaz

museums of ❺ Cetinje ➤ p. 84 you can learn about the country's history and discover the magnificent old embassy buildings. On the gigantic relief map in the Biljarda museum you can even get a bird's eye perspective of Montenegro.

COUNTLESS SCENIC VIEWS

A detour takes you on the well-marked route to the Lovćen National Park and the large ❻ Njegoš Mausoleum ➤ p. 87. From the nearby viewing platform, on clear days you can see as far as the mountains of Albania. Back in Cetinje, *you continue on the M2-3 in the direction of Budva.* On the other side of the mountain, quite unexpectedly, there is a far-reaching view of the Adriatic. *Drive onwards on the E80 past Budva and towards Tivat. After the mountain and about 3km further on, take the turning to* ❼ Jaz ➤ p. 68. At the eastern end of the 1,200m-long beach is the Hotel Poseidon *(poseidon-jaz.com).* Enjoy a swim and the evening sunset and stay overnight here.

A picturesque stop: Rose in the Bay of Kotor

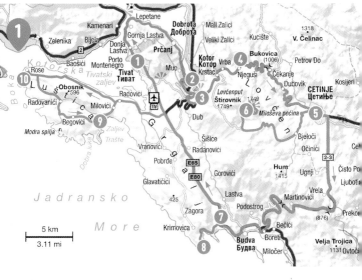

COOL ON THE BEACH

The country road continues past the Bay of Trsteno and onwards to the trendy beach of ⑧ Ploče *with pools, cocktail bars, rock and electro music. For the young people here, swimming is not top of the agenda, even if the deep blue sea does beckon.* Back on the E80 in the direction of Tivat, turn off before the airport and head for the country road to Radovići and the sophisticated ⑨ Almara Beach ➤ p. 59 to relax beneath a parasol.

ROMANTIC VILLAGES & A CHIC MARINA

Now you can explore the Luštica Peninsula. *The country road heads back to Radovići and, shortly before the coast, you turn left to Krašići. You then get to Klinci from where the road winds downhill to* ⑩ Rose ➤ p. 61. Take a stroll through this idyllic artist village and enjoy the view over the Bay of Kotor. *Then the coastal road leads through olive groves and deserted villages. Follow the signs to the airport, and head back to* ① Tivat and the marina of Porto Montenegro. Finish your tour at the One - Restaurant & Bar ➤ p. 59 which serves Mediterranean food with views of the luxury yachts.

DAY 2

⑧ **Ploče**

28km 30 mins

⑨ **Almara Beach**

18km 30 mins

⑩ **Rose**

32km 45 mins

① **Tivat**

❷ HIGH-FLYERS IN HIKING BOOTS

➤ Hike through dense primeval forest in the Biogradska gora National Park
➤ Listen to wolves howling in the distance
➤ See for yourself why the lakes here are called the "Eyes of the Mountains"

📍	Kolašin	🏁	Kolašin
↻	Approx. 39km	🚶	2 days (16 hrs total walking time)
▮▮▮	Difficult	↗	1,000m

ℹ️ What to pack: helmet, hiking boots, warm clothing (temperature in summer: 12–15°C), picnic.
Important tips: confirm the details in advance with the tour operator **Eco-Tours** *(see p. 116 | eco-tours.co.me).* These include guide, overnight stay before, during and after the hike *(only possible May–Nov),* pickup from Lake Biogradsko (approx. 20km) with your own car or a hire car. Although all the trails are well marked, you should not set off without a guide!

DAY 1
❶ Kolašin

11km 4½ hrs

❷ Ćirilovac Monastery

4km 2¾ hrs

❸ Ključ

MONTENEGRO'S FLORA

Starting in ❶ Kolašin ➤ p. 114, walk from your accommodation, Bijeli Potok, *along the road in the direction of Dulovine as far as the outskirts of town.* A signpost marks the way to the Botanical Garden that offers you a first glimpse of the mountain wildflowers. *A gravel road continues in the direction of Izlasci into the mountains, partly along a stream and through increasingly dense forest. Past Izlasci you reach* ❷ Ćirilovac Monastery. In the main church, light a candle according to the Orthodox custom, and make a wish. Then, it's time for a refreshing picnic.

PICK BERRIES IN BEAR COUNTRY

On forest footpaths continue hiking uphill towards ❸ Mount Ključ (1,973m). In summer, you cross

---

fragrant meadows and can pick forest berries, and in late autumn you can hear the distant howl of wolves. The region is renowned for the wolves and brown bears that live off the beaten tracks. Walk to the summit and the chapel. Here, you have a panoramic view of the mountains of northeast Montenegro.

A DRINK ON THE ALP

The higher you climb on the footpath, the more frequently you encounter the *katuni*, or mountain huts, some of which are still open for light snacks. By the time you reach the summer pasture, or *katun* ④ Krivi Do, you will have earned a break. Here, you should try the home-produced cheeses *lisnati sir* and *kajmak*. It's best to drink the *rakija* (fruit brandy) slowly and with a glass of water so that the spirits don't burn your throat. Then, continue climbing even higher to 1,750m to *katun* ⑤ Vranjak, and stay overnight in a wooden hut.

"EYE OF THE MOUNTAIN"

Next morning, *descend in the direction of the lake. From the summit of* ⑥ Donji Lumer you have an amazing view of Lake Biogradsko. At the *katun* ⑦ Goleš, at

5km 1¾ hrs

④ Krivi Do

5km 1¾ hrs

⑤ Vranjak

DAY 2

9km 3hrs

⑥ Donji Lumer

1.5km 30 mins

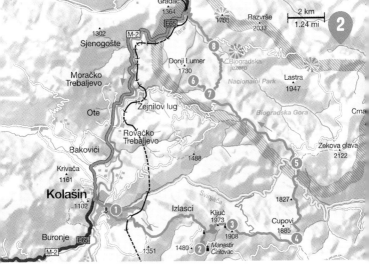

an altitude of 1,600m, along with sheep, goats, barking dogs and birdsong you are greeted by exceptional cuisine made with regional ingredients: lamb boiled in milk or roasted in hot ashes, corn hash, thick yogurt and freshly baked bread that is still warm.

INSIDER TIP
Tasty mountain food

PADDLE ON THE LAKE

After the meal, you can rent a boat at the *katun* and *then descend through the primeval forest to* ⑧ Lake Biogradsko ➤ p. 116. Having reached the end of your hiking tour, you deserve a rest, while you paddle gently across the water. A driver will collect you for the return journey to ⓪ Kolašin (as arranged in advance with Eco-Tours).

⑧ Lake Biogradsko
20km 20 mins
⓪ Kolašin

❸ OLIVES, PELICANS AND LUNAR LANDSCAPES

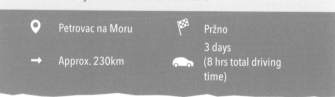
➤ Admire an ancient olive tree
➤ Sail past pelicans and cormorants
➤ Get a bird's-eye view of the Budva Riviera

📍 Petrovac na Moru	🏁 Pržno
➡ Approx. 230km	3 days 🚗 (8 hrs total driving time)

MARKET FRUIT AND MOCHA

Your day starts off in ① Petrovac na Moru ➤ p. 71 with a swim and a walk through the fragrant pine forest to the beach at Lučice. *Next, on the E80, head for* ② Bar ➤ p. 75, and ejoy the shopping experience at the farmers' market. Walk to the harbour and watch the large ferries and container ships. In ③ Stari Bar ➤ p. 76 stroll through the centuries-old ruins and surrender to the temptation of delicacies from the Turkish patisserie Karaduzović. A mocha goes perfectly with a sweet baklava.

DAY 1
① Petrovac na Moru
20km 20 mins
② Bar
③ Stari Bar

Hiking in the Biogradska gora National Park brings you closer to heaven

On the E851 in the direction of Ulcinj, just before you reach the village of Tomba (the route is marked) you will pass an ancient ④ olive tree ➤ p. 76. The 2,200-year-old tree is among the oldest in the world and is an amazing sight.

SWIM BY THE ROCKY COAST

In ⑤ Ulcinj ➤ p. 76 you will meet your hostess for the night at the friendly Lungo Mare apartments (mobile 067 63 69 20). Close to your accommodation, near the Hotel Albatros, the cliff-side beaches are hidden away in dense pine forests. After a quick swim, walk on a footpath along the city beach into the old town. On the terrace of the Kulla e Balshajve hotel (mobile 067 01 77 15 | hotelkullaebalshajve.com), enjoy the excellent fish dishes and the view over Ulcinj. And if you want to find a souvenir, the region's best silversmiths are at Ulica zlatara, and for olive oil you can't beat Olive Ponte (Rr. Ymer Prizreni | oliveponte.com).

MOUNTAIN LEG TO LAKE SKADAR

Shortly after Krute, turn left off the E851 and on to the R16 in the direction of Virpazar. The impressive summits of Mount Rumija accompany the journey, and

2km 5 mins

④ Olive tree

23km 25 mins

⑤ Ulcinj

DAY 2

38km 1 hr

⑥ Ostroš
18km 20 mins

⑦ Murići
1km 5 mins

⑧ Beška
23km 35 mins

⑨ Virpazar

soon Lake Skadar glimmers on your right. *You pass small villages like* ⑥ Ostroš, *where Catholic churches stand alongside mosques. Drive to* ⑦ Murići ➤ p. 91. The lower part of the village of Donji Murići is situated on a bay of Lake Skadar. After a swim, enjoy fresh fish at the restaurant Izletište Murići *(mobile 069 68 82 88 | €)*. Here, you can book a boat trip to visit the nuns on the island of ⑧ Beška ➤ p. 91. *Continue by car to* ⑨ Virpazar ➤ p. 89, *where you can stay overnight in the* Guesthouse Vukasevic *(see also booking.com)*. First, walk to the visitor centre to book a boat trip to Rijeka Crnojevića for the next morning.

DAY 3

WATER LILIES FOR EARLY BIRDS

Early risers are rewarded with one of the most fabulous excursions that Lake Skadar has to offer: the two-hour return boat trip to Rijeka Crnojevića starts at 6am. You glide among water lilies to the river of the same name that meanders through the countryside like a fjord. Look out for pelicans and cormorants, storks and falcons.

UNFORGETTABLE VIEWS

Back in the car enjoy the unforgettable view from high above of the meandering watercourse, *when you drive on the R16 to Rijeka Crnojevića. Shortly before the village follow the signposted country road to Gornji Ceklin* to the ⑩ Vukmirović farm. Watch as the beekeeper extracts the honey and enjoy a light snack. *The M2-3 heads towards the coast. In Obzovica, leave the motorway for the country road in the direction of Utrg and Brčeli and head for the M2 in the direction of Petrovac.* The barren mountains in this region are reminiscent of a lunar landscape. At the summit, the view of the Budva Riviera stretching out before you is quite breathtaking.

⑩ Vukmirović farm
61km 1 hr

Descend through the hairpin bends and the travel along the E80 to ⑪ Sv. Stefan ➤ p. 70. Enjoy a meal in the Olive restaurant and admire the view of the beautiful, rocky island. Round off the tour with a walk along the stunning nearby bays of ⑫ Miločer ➤ p. 71 and ⑬ Pržno ➤ p. 69.

⑪ Sv. Stefan
1km 20 mins

⑫ Miločer
0.5km 10 mins

⑬ Pržno

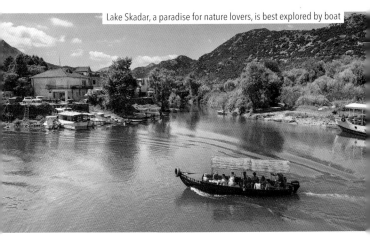
Lake Skadar, a paradise for nature lovers, is best explored by boat

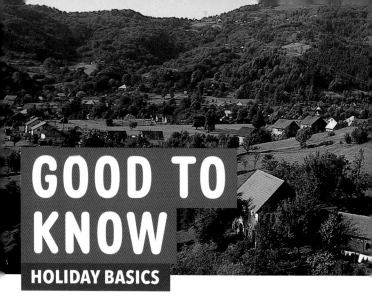

GOOD TO KNOW
HOLIDAY BASICS

ARRIVAL

GETTING THERE

From the ferry terminal in Calais (France) you can start by taking the A26 through France, the A25 through Belgium and Luxembourg or the A16 through Belgium, then cross Germany, Austria, Slovenia and Croatia to get to Montenegro. The drive to Tivat takes about 22 hours. Ferries from Dover to Calais and back run many times a day.

The Channel Tunnel connects the United Kingdom and France. There are train connections between London St Pancras and Paris or Brussels (Belgium). Trains depart from several destinations in Europe for Belgrade; this is the unavoidable stopover before travelling on to Montenegro. You then continue on via Bijelo Polje, Mojkovac, Kolašin and Podgorica to Bar on the Adriatic. The landscape along this route is one of the most impressive in the Balkans.

There is a well-developed bus network linking Montenegro to Europe via Dubrovnik or Belgrade.

WizzAir *(wizzair.com)* operates direct flights from the UK, otherwise you will have one stop en route. Air Montenegro *(airmontenegro.com/en)* flies to Tivat and Podgorica from several European destinations. Air Serbia *(airserbia.com)* serves numerous international destinations from Belgrade with connecting flights to Tivat and Podgorica. It is also possible to fly to Dubrovnik and then take a taxi to Montenegro.

GETTING IN

Visas are not required for those arriving from the UK, EU and the USA for stays of up to 90 days. Your passport should be issued in the last ten years and be valid for at least three months

The train journey to Bar offers great scenic views

after your planned date of departure from Montenegro. On entering Montenegro, make sure the border police put an entry stamp in your passport. This helps avoid problems related to verifying the length of your stay in the country.

CLIMATE & WHEN TO GO

In July and August when the temperatures on the coast can soar to 40°C (or higher in the valley around Podgorica) it will still be about 20°C in the Durmitor Mountains. Winters are mild on the coast and harsh in the mountains. The best months for a beach holiday are May/June and September/October. The extreme heat and overcrowded beaches in the school holidays can make a visit stressful during the months of July and August. The temperature of the sea is more than 20°C by June and can reach 29°C at the end of the season. There is a good deal of snow in the mountains between December and March and the skiing season in most resorts lasts from November to April.

GETTING AROUND

CAR HIRE

International and national car hire agencies have branches in most of the major holiday resorts. Travel agencies will also take care of bookings. Good comparison websites include *rental-cars.com* and *autoeurope.eu*. Sometimes you can hire a car for 20 euros per day or less.

DRIVING

National registration papers and driving licenses are recognised. It is obligatory to have a green international insurance card and you will need to show it at the border when you enter the country. Maximum speed limits are: 50 kmh in built-up areas; 80 kmh on country roads; 100 kmh on motorways. Vehicles with trailers are not allowed to exceed 80 kmh.

The legal alcohol limit for drivers is set at 0.3g/kg. You must drive with dipped headlights at all times. High-vis vests are mandatory as is a fire extinguisher. Driving without sturdy footwear is prohibited.

Traffic fines are heavy in Montenegro: overtake in a tunnel or run a red light and you will lose your license; telephoning in the car – 30 euros; driving without wearing a seatbelt – 20 euros. You should contact the police immediately if you have an accident. The emergency service *(tel. 1 98 07)* will provide assistance if you have a breakdown on the road.

The country's first-ever motorway, which was completed only recently, surrounds the capital at a length of 41km, and more sections are planned. The coastal road between Herceg Novi and Ulcinj as well as roads from the coast to Podgorica and Cetinje are generally busy in high season. You can therefore expect long delays. The Sozina Tunnel on the E80 between Podgorica and Bar charges tolls *(2.50 euros/car)*. Parking fees are extremely high on the coast – up to 15 euros a day – and there is usually no guarantee given for the safety of your car.

PUBLIC TRANSPORT

An extensive bus network connects all the major cities and there are also several lines that run regularly between the main destinations on the coast. Tickets can be purchased at the bus terminals *(autobuska stanica)* or from the driver and are inexpensive when compared with tariffs in the rest of Europe.

The train from Bar to Belgrade *(zcg-prevoz.me)* makes stops in Sutomore, Podgorica, Kolašin, Mojkovac and Bijelo Polje every day.

EMERGENCIES

EMBASSIES
BRITISH EMBASSY
Ulcinjska 8 | Podgorica 81000 | tel. +382 (0)20 42 01 00 | gov.uk/world/ montenegro

FESTIVALS & EVENTS
ALL YEAR ROUND

FEBRUARY
Mimosa Festival (Herceg Novi): The first mimosa blossoms are greeted with fanfare on the waterfront promenade | *hercegnovi.travel* (photo)
Carnival (all over): Masked balls and parades along the coast | *kotor.travel*

APRIL
HAPS Theatre Festival (Herceg Novi), *hercegfest.me*
International Jazz Day: Concerts in ten towns | *jazzday.com*

MAY
Montenegro Cup (Kotor and Nikšić): Free climbers shin up the steep cliffs in Kotor and Nikšić in their attempts to win the cup.
Night of the Museums (19 May): Free entry to dozens of museums across the country.

JUNE
International Children's Carnival (Herceg Novi): See p. 48.

JULY
Olive Festival (Tivat): See p. 60.
Festival of Male Choirs "klapa" (Perast): A cappella groups of up to eight singers | *festivalklapaperast.com*
International Fashion Festival (Porto Montenegro, Tivat): Fashion show for all | *portomontenegro.com/events*
Days of Tara (Mojkovac): Daredevils jump off the Tara Bridge into the river below | *mojkovac.travel*

AUGUST
Film Festival (Herceg Novi): Open-air cinema, sometimes with English subtitles | *FB: Montenegro Film Festival*
Sea Dance Festival (Buljarica Beach, Budva): See p. 68.

OCTOBER
Halloween (Budva): Witches and elves take over for one day.

DECEMBER
New Year's Eve Concerts: In many towns and cities just before midnight.

UNITED STATES EMBASSY

Džona Džeksona 2 | Podgorica 81000 | tel. +382 (0)20 41 05 00 | me.usembassy.gov

EMERGENCY SERVICES

It is best to call the general Europe-wide emergency number *112.* Otherwise call:

Police: *tel. 122*
Fire brigade: *tel. 123*
Ambulance: *tel. 124*
Mountain rescue: *tel. 040 25 60 84.*
If you do not have a Montenegrin SIM card, include the country code *00382.*

HEALTH

There are state-run clinics in almost every town or village, and they are marked with a red cross. You will have to pay for any treatment you receive and it is therefore a good idea to have foreign travel health insurance with the option of repatriation. Private clinics have been established in the larger towns. The tourist offices can give you the addresses of local doctors – most of them speak English. The well-stocked pharmacies can provide help for minor mishaps.

ESSENTIALS

ACCOMMODATION

Good hotels are expensive, but nice, reasonably priced private accommodation can still be found. There is a great difference in the prices charged along the coast: Herceg Novi, Budva and Perast are the most expensive.

INSIDER TIP
More Adriatic for your money

Things start to get cheaper after you leave Petrovac and head towards Ulcinj. Prices often fall by up to 40 per cent in the off peak seasons. The booking website *booking.com* plays a big role because private offers including amazing apartments and guesthouses now exclusively use this website or *airbnb.com.*

HOW MUCH DOES IT COST

Ice cream	*1 euro* *for one ball of home-made ice cream*
Snack	*3 euros* *for a ćevapčići snack*
Coffee	*2 euros* *for a cappuccino*
Petrol	*1.30 euros* *for 1 litre super*
Bus fare	*3 euros* *for the journey from Budva to Petrovac (approx. 20km)*
Kayak hire	*15 euros* *for 3 hrs in the Bay of Kotor*

CAMPING

Campsites are known as *kampovi* or *auto kampovi.* They are always well equipped. *camping.info/montenegro*

CUSTOMS

It is permitted to bring currency up to 10,000 euros into or out of the country. Apart from food that is destined for your own consumption, it is prohibited to import food with the exception of dried fruit, tea and coffee up to a total weight of 1kg, 2 litres of juice and 5 litres of water. In addition, 2 litres of alcohol up to 22 per cent or 1 litre of spirits over 22 per cent and 200 cigarettes or 50 cigars or 250g of tobacco can be imported duty free. For tax and duty on goods brought to the UK, go to *gov.uk/bringing-goods-into-uk-personal-use*.

LANGUAGE

Although English is the best language for getting around, not everybody speaks it. If you speak Russian, you may tentatively ask if people would like to talk to you in that language because some may well agree.

It can be difficult to search for a particular route in Montenegro. In this travel guide and on websites, the routes are easy to follow, as they are in Latin script, but the local road names are only written in Cyrillic text. The best option is often to ask. In the south and northeast of Montenegro, Albanian is a second official language after Montenegrin. The road signs are therefore bilingual, e.g. the town Ulcinj is also called Ulqin.

The abbreviation Sv. stands for the Montenegrin forms of the word "saint", i.e. *Sveti* (masculine) and *Sveta* (feminine).

MONEY & CURRENCY

Although Montenegro is still not a member of the EU, it has unilaterally introduced the euro as its currency. Cash machines issue normal euro notes for a charge.

The daily limit for withdrawals from a cash machine is 700 euros. Hotels and supermarkets accept all standard credit cards (MasterCard, Visa) but you should ask beforehand in restaurants and small shops.

NUDIST BEACHES

One of the few nudist beaches in Montenegro is on the island of Ada Bojana near Ulcinj. A small rock is reserved for naturists in Ulcinj itself. The small Nijivce nudist beach is located at the outermost tip of Igalo. Fishing boats take tourists from other resorts to small bays where they can bathe nude. Ask on site!

OPENING HOURS

There are no fixed opening hours and some shops and restaurants stay open until midnight in summer. The following applies to the restaurants mentioned in this guide: if not stated otherwise, they are open daily both for lunch and dinner. Many public offices close at 4pm. Post offices are open from 7am–8pm on weekdays and sometimes longer during the tourist season.

PRICES

Imported food, in particular, is now almost as expensive as it is in Western Europe, but local produce in the market is cheaper. Petrol is also expensive. Prices vary throughout the country: for example, many products are cheaper in Bar than in Budva. As a rule, life in the interior is cheaper than on the coast. The sun loungers you hire on the beaches can also be expensive. It is common to pay around 10 euros per day and you can pay up to 100 euros for a luxurious bed shaded by a canopy on the beach.

PUBLIC HOLIDAYS

1/2 Jan	New Year
6–8 Jan	Orthodox Christmas
April/May	Orthodox Good Friday
April/May	Orthodox Easter Monday
1/2 May	Labour Day
21/22 May	Independence Day
13/14 July	Statehood Day

TELEPHONE & WIFI
All hotels have WiFi, as do most campsites and private accommodation. Cafés post signs if they have a WiFi hotspot and some restaurants and pubs provide internet access. You can even get WiFi in hire cars for a surcharge. As a rule: the larger the town, the better the internet connection.

If you want to use your mobile with your home SIM card, we recommend that you contact your network provider for their roaming charges. Montenegro is not yet an EU member state, which means that roaming might be expensive. If in doubt, deactivate mobile data as soon as you arrive.

If you do intend to use your mobile phone in Montenegro, you can buy a prepaid card with a Montenegrin number. Take a sim lock-free smartphone with you and simply buy a prepaid deal at a newspaper stand or in the supermarket. There are special deals at reduced prices for tourists

INSIDER TIP
Surf like the locals

(e.g. *turistički pripejd paket* by T-Mobile).

If you are making a call within Montenegro, dial the area code or mobile phone code, which always begins with zero, and then the contact number. For calls from your home country to Montenegro and vice versa, dial the international dialling code followed by the area or mobile phone code, but omit the first zero and then dial the contact number. International dialling codes: United Kingdom *0044*, Canada and USA *001*, Australia *0061*, Montenegro *00382*.

TIPPING
It is customary to round up small amounts in cafés. However, in restaurants tourists should leave a tip of 10–15 percent of the bill.

TOURIST INFORMATION
Nacionalna turistička organizacija Crne Gore (NTO) *(Slobode 2 | Podgorica | tel. 077 10 00 01 | 24-hr information line 08000 13 00 | montenegro.travel),* the National Tourist Organisation of Montenegro, has branches throughout the country. There are also travel agencies in almost every town.

Nacionalni Parkovi Crne Gore (Trg Vojvode Bećir-Bega Osmanagića 16 | Podgorica | tel. 020 60 10 15 | nparkovi.me) will provide information on Montenegro's national parks.

TOURIST TAX
The general tourist tax of approx. 1 euro per person per day is usually included in the price of your accommodation.

Campsite on the shore of Lake Plav

WEATHER IN BUDVA

High season
Low season

	JAN	FEB	MARCH	APRIL	MAY	JUNE	JULY	AUG	SEPT	OCT	NOV	DEC
Daytime temperature	3°	3°	15°	18°	22°	26°	29°	29°	26°	22°	15°	5°
Night-time temperature	-3°	-2°	6°	10°	14°	18°	20°	20°	17°	13°	8°	0°
☀	3	4	5	7	9	10	11	11	8	7	4	3
🌧	14	13	12	13	14	13	9	9	8	11	14	14
≈	13°	13°	14°	15°	17°	22°	23°	25°	22°	20°	18°	15°

☀ Hours of sunshine per day   🌧 Rainy days per month   ≈ Sea temperature in °C

WORDS & PHRASES IN MONTENEGRIN

SMALL TALK

yes/no/maybe	**da/ne/možda**
please/thank you	**molim/hvala**
Good morning/Good afternoon/Good evening/Goodnight	**Dobro jutro/Dobar dan/Dobro veče/Laku noć**
Hello/Goodbye	**Zdravo/Doviđenja**
Bye!	**Zdravo!/Ciao!**
My name is …	**Zovem se …**
What is your name? (formal/informal)	**Kako se zovete?/Kako se zoveš?**
I come from …	**Dolazim iz …**
Sorry!/Excuse me!	**Oprosti (Izvini)!/Pardon!/Oprostite (Izvinite)!**
Sorry, what did you say?	**Molim?**
I (don't) like this	**To mi se (ne) sviđa**
I want …/Do you have …?	**Želim …/Da li imate?**
May I take a photo of you?	**Da li smem da Vas fotografišem?**

SYMBOLS

EATING & DRINKING

The menu, please	**Jelovnik, (meni) molim**
Please could I have ...?	**Molim vas, htio (f htjela) bih ...?**
bottle/carafe/glass	**bocu/bokal/čašu**
knife/fork/spoon	**nož/viljušku/kašiku**
with/without gas	**gazirana/negazirana**
vegetarian/allergy	**vegetarijanac (f vegetarijanka)/ alergija**
I would like to pay, please	**Molim vas, htio (f htjela) bih da platim**
invoice/receipt/tip	**račun/priznanica/bakšiš**
cash/debit card/credit card	**keš/elektronska kartica/kreditna kartica**

MISCELLANEOUS

Where is ...? Where are ...?	**Gdje je ...?/Gdje su ...?**
How much does it cost?	**Koliko košta?**
Where can I get internet access?	**Gdje ću naći internet-vezu?**
What time is it?	**Je sati?**
today/tomorrow/yesterday	**danas/sjutra/juče**
Monday/Tuesday/Wednesday/ Thursday/Friday/Saturday/Sunday/ holiday	**ponedjeljak/utorak/srijeda/ četvrtak/petak/subota/ edjelja/praznik**
open/closed	**otvoreno/zatvoreno**
timetable/ticket	**red vožnje/biljet, karta**
fever/pain/diarrhoea/nausea	**groznica/bolovi/proliv, dijareja/ mučnina**
hospital/accident & emergency/ pharmacy	**bolnica/urgentni centar/apoteka**
broken/not working	**nije ispravno**
breakdown/mechanic	**kvar/automehaničarska radionica**
prohibition/forbidden/danger/ dangerous	**zabrana/zabranjeno/opasnost/ opasno**
Help!/Look out!/Be careful!	**Upomoć!/Pažnja!/Oprez!**
0/1/2/3/4/5/6/7/8/9/10/ 100/1,000	**nula/jedan (f jedna, n jedno)/dva (f dvije)/tri/četiri/pet/šest/sedam/ osam/devet/deset/sto, stotina/ hiljadu**

HOLIDAY VIBES
FOR RELAXATION & CHILLING

FOR BOOKWORMS & FILM BUFFS

📖 ENCYCLOPEDIA OF THE DEAD
Danilo Kiš (1935–89) is considered to be one of the most important writers in the Balkans. His parables on life, love and death made him famous and most of his books have been published in English, such as this volume of short stories from 1983.

🎥 BROTHERS BLOOM
Rian Johnson directed this caper comedy drama (2008) which is partly set in Montenegro and stars Rachel Weisz, Mark Ruffalo and Adrien Brody. The beach shots of the Adriatic alone will make you want more of the country!

🎥 THE NOVEMBER MAN
The 2014 spy action thriller isn't exactly a reinvention of this genre, but it is definitely captivating, and that's mainly due to leading man Pierce Brosnan. A lot of the filming took place in Montenegro, and in chic Herceg Novi in particular.

📖 BRIDGE OVER THE DRINA
In 1961, Ivo Andrić (1892–1975) won the Nobel Prize for Literature for his story about the stone bridge that was built over the River Drina during the Turkish era. The author spent the last years of his life in Herceg Novi.

PLAYLIST

0:58

‖ PERPER – MONTENEGRO JAZZ
A legendary band from Cetinje. Although the title of this hit refers to "jazz", it is actually a rock song.

▶ WHO SEE FEAT. SMOKE MARDELJANO – NE BIH SE MIJENJA
Good rap in Montenegrin plus full-bodied reggae rhythms – the sound is great even if you can't understand it!

▶ NINA PETKOVIĆ – DANCE TILL I DIE
Spirited electronic dancefloor music with Balkan sounds.

▶ KNEZ – ADIO
The mixture of pop and tear-jerker landed Knez 13th place at the 2015 Eurovision Song Contest.

▶ NINA ŽIŽIĆ – KISS YOU GOODBYE
Few Montenegrin artists perform in English, but this pop ballader makes a lovely exception.

*Your holiday soundtrack is available on **Spotify** under **MARCO POLO** Montenegro*

Or scan this code with the Spotify app

DISCOVER-MONTENEGRO.COM
Information on the culture and history, geography and nature of Montenegro. Also tips for activities and many photos.

TWOWANDERINGSOLES.COM/ MONTENEGRO
Katie and Ben from Minnesota (USA) use their travel blog to showcase their personal "Best of Montenegro", including wonderful photographs.

FACEBOOK: BUDVA
This Facebook site does not only show pictures of Budva but all Montenegro.

Interesting links and videos are also posted here.

NATIONAL PARKS OF MONTENEGRO
App for the country's five national parks, with interactive maps, virtual tours, photo galleries and event info.

VISIT-MONTENEGRO.COM
All you need to know about your destination at a glance: interactive maps with planning function, a link to a video channel with videos about Montenegro, online booking services and much more.

TRAVEL PURSUIT

THE MARCO POLO HOLIDAY QUIZ

Do you know what makes Montenegro tick? Test your knowledge of the idiosyncrasies and eccentricities of the country and its people. You will find the answers below, with further details on pages 20–25 of this guide.

❶ When does Ostrog Monastery celebrate the feast day of St Vasilije?
a) 12 June
b) 12 May
c) 12 April

❷ Which country did Montenegro separate from by means of a referendum?
a) Croatia
b) Bosnia
c) Serbia

❸ Which ethnic minority lives in Montenegro's south and northeast?
a) Albanians
b) Kosovars
c) Serbs

❹ What is the name of the literary masterpiece by Petrović Njegoš, the people's poet?
a) The Mountain Peace
b) The Mountain Cross
c) The Mountain Wreath

❺ What name is given to Montenegro's traditional clans?
a) *pleme*
b) *bratstvo*
c) *gilde*

❻ Which country has fewer citizens than Montenegro?
a) Latvia
b) Cape Verde
c) El Salvador

Correct answers: 1b, 2c, 3a, 4c, 5a, 6b, 7b, 8c, 9b, 10a, 11a, 12c

A monument to Montenegro's great poet: the Njegoš Mausoleum

❼ Since when has Montenegro been using the euro?
a) 2000
b) 2002
c) The euro is not yet Montenegro's currency.

❽ And which currency was the country's unofficial parallel currency for many years?
a) Russian rouble
b) Swiss frank
c) Deutsche Mark

❾ How do you pronounce Montenegro's Slavic name?
a) Tschrna Gora
b) Tsrna Gora
c) Tsrngr

❿ What do Montenegrins call Mount Lovćen?
a) Olympus
b) Acropolis
c) Heaven's Gate

⓫ Apart from "mountain", what else can *gora* mean?
a) forest
b) confederation
c) alliance of the brave

⓬ Which alphabet is used in Montenegro?
a) Latin alphabet
b) Greek alphabet
c) Cyrillic alphabet

INDEX

CHEQUERED HISTORY & TESTIMONIES IN STONE

The fate of this small country has repeatedly been determined by European powers. These cultural influences are immediately apparent in the impressive architecture of *Kotor's old town* (photo).
➤ p. 51, Bay of Kotor

TRADITIONAL LAMB

In Cetinje, at the *Belveder* restaurant, you can feast on a traditional Montenegrin delicacy: lamb, braised in a ceramic pot on the open fire. Key to its success is that even the lid, called *sač*, is covered in embers.
➤ p. 86, Cetinje, Lake Skadar & Podgorica

MONUMENT ON THE SUMMIT

The Montenegrins fervently revere their national heroes, and they have placed a colossal monument to the greatest on one of the highest mountains in the country. The poet Prince Njegoš lies in the *mausoleum* on the Jezerski vrh peak, with stunning views of Lovćen National Park.
➤ p. 87, Cetinje, Lake Skadar & Podgorica

ADVENTUROUS & SCENIC DRIVE

The 76km-long *Durmitor Ring* leads through the national park's spectacular mountains on narrow, and in parts steep, tarmacked roads, and finally to the incredible viewpoint of the Tara Canyon.
➤ p. 105, The Northwest

COFFEE TRADITION

No day is complete without a mocha in Montenegro! The locals drink coffee in the mornings, at midday, in the evenings, during breaks, and before and after meals. Try a cup in the *Sugar Resto Cafe* in Bijelo Polje, where they also serve delicious cakes.
➤ p. 113, The Northeast

GET TO KNOW MONTE-NEGRO

Take yourself back to Montenegro's seafaring past, when ships set sail from Peras

INDEX & CREDITS

WE WANT TO HEAR FROM YOU!

Did you have a great holiday? Is there something on your mind? Whatever it is, let us know! Whether you want to praise the guide, alert us to errors or give us a personal tip – MARCO POLO would be pleased to hear from you. Please contact us by email:

We do everything we can to provide the very latest information for your trip. Nevertheless, despite all of our authors' thorough research, errors can creep in. MARCO POLO does not accept any liability for this.

sales@heartwoodpublishing.co.uk

PICTURE CREDITS

Cover photo: Bay of Kotor, Perast (AWL Images: A. Copson)
Photos: R. Freyer (128/129); Getty Images: S. Condrea (22), Istankov (86); Huber-images: J. Huber (8/9, 70, 73, 74), S. Kremer (51, 52), A. Pavan (138/139), D. Pearson (2/3), S. Surac (89, 90); Huber-images/4Corner Images (95); M. Kaupat (143); G. Knoll (12, 77); Laif: M. Cavalier (back cover flap), Henseler (55), K. Henseler (40/41), F. Heuer (11, 58, 103, 117), T. & B. Morandi (66, 80/81, 92), Zahn (140/141); Laif/Haytham-Rea: L Cousin (47); Laif/robertharding: S. Black (79), F. Fell (69); Lookphotos: G. Bayerl (62/63); mauritius images: M. Siepmann (2/3, 56/57, 106), S. Kolesnyk (14/15, 16/17, 21, 96/97); mauritius images/age fotostock: K. Zelazowski (49); mauritius images/Alamy (100, F. Brilli (61), S. Day (28/29, 29), eFesenko (44), D. Fiore (34/35), O. Kachmar (118/119), B. Klement (125), S. Milenkovic (26/27), V. Nadtochii (outside front cover flap, inside front cover flap1), B. Stefanovic (33, 131); mauritius images/Alamy/HDesert (32/33); mauritius images/Alamy/Vita (36); mauritius images/Alamy/Zoonar GmbH (112); mauritius images/Aurora RF: M. Radovanovic (24); mauritius images/Hemis.fr: R. Mattes (6/7); mauritius images/imagebroker (114); mauritius images/Pixtal (13); mauritius images/RnDmS/Alamy (10, 108/109); mauritius images/Westend61: E. Strigl (84); mauritius images/Westend61RF: M. Siepmann (104/105, 120); mauritius images/Zoonar/Alamy (127); Andrew Mayovskyy/Shutterstock (6/7); Sergey Lyashenko/Shutterstock (135)

3rd Edition – fully revised and updated 2024
Worldwide Distribution: Heartwood Publishing Ltd, Bath, United Kingdom
www.heartwoodpublishing.co.uk

Authors: Danja Antonović, Mirko Kaupat
Editor: Franziska Kahl
Picture editor: Gabriele Forst
Cartography: © MAIRDUMONT, Ostfildern (38–39, 121, 123, 126, outer wallet, pull-out map); © MAIRDUMONT, Ostfildern, using data from OpenStreetMap, licence CC-BY-SA 2.0 (42–43, 64–65, 82–83, 98–99, 110–111)
Cover design and pull-out map cover design: bilekjaeger_Kreativagentur with Zukunftswerkstatt, Stuttgart
Page design: Langenstein Communication GmbH, Ludwigsburg

Heartwood Publishing credits:
Translated from the German by Thomas Moser, Robert Scott McInnes, Jozef van der Voort
Editors: Rosamund Sales, Kate Michell, Felicity Laughton, Sophie Blacksell Jones
Prepress: Summerlane Books, Bath
Printed in India

All rights reserved. No part of this book may be reproduced, stored in a retrieval system or transmitted in any form or by any means (electronic, mechanical, photocopying, recording or otherwise) without prior written permission from the publisher.

MARCO POLO AUTHOR
MIRKO KAUPAT
Years ago, when journalist Mirco Kaupat was travelling on one of Montenegro's narrow, poorly maintained mountain roads, he momentarily wished that he was in the Caribbean or some other sunny place, but then the clouds parted to reveal Lake Skadar – and all his troubles were forgotten. Mirko Kaupat has had many such experiences in this small but fabulous country.

DOS & DON'TS

HOW TO AVOID SLIP-UPS & BLUNDERS

DO AGREE ON A RATE FOR YOUR TAXI
A taxi meter plays no role – the price you agree on before you set out is the real charge – so before you get into a taxi you must negotiate the fare. Most of the drivers speak a smattering of English. Make sure that you choose a registered taxi, not a private provider.

DON'T DRINK TAP WATER
Although plumbing is improving in the country, the water in many towns and villages – especially on the coast – is not safe to drink. It is best to play it safe and stick to bottled mineral water.

DO STICK TO THE SPEED LIMIT
When buses and trucks hold up traffic and you are stuck behind them, try to relax and drive carefully – the winding roads in the mountains of Montenegro require your concentration. You must not overtake school buses when children are getting on or off. Also, there are a surprising number of speed cameras and police checkpoints.

DO WEAR APPROPRIATE CLOTHES
If you visit a church or monastery, make sure that you are not too casually dressed – shorts are not acceptable. By the way, members of the Orthodox faith exit religious places backwards – with their eyes fixed on the icons.

DON'T UNDERESTIMATE THE "BLACK MOUNTAIN"
The mountainous north is still something of an insider's tip. However, the weather can be unpredictable at an altitude of 1,500m and the trails are not always well marked. It is a good idea to hike in groups of at least three and take a mountain guide with you. Always make sure you let the people you are staying with know where you are going.